He Teaches My Hands to War

Larry Stockstill

Bethany World Prayer Center
Baker, Louisiana

Contents

Chapter 1

Understanding Spiritual Warfare

"War is cruelty, and you cannot refine it." So said William Tecumseh Sherman, Union general during the U.S. Civil War. In its simplicity, that brief phrase sums up the innate horror and terror of war. No matter how just the cause or unavoidable the fight, the fact remains that war is utterly destructive and unbearably painful. The casualties are great—sometimes even extreme—and the price, though it may be possible to justify it, is so high that no rational being ever enters war lightly. It is a tactic of last resort, engaged in only after all other avenues of peace have been exhausted.

Human beings are all too familiar with the tragedy of war. It has been a part of the human record from the beginning of time. Countless young wives have sent their husbands off to war with a kiss on the mouth and a hope in the heart for their safe return, while thousands upon thousands have endured the agony of losing the dearest, most precious thing in their lives. Its cost on humankind has been incalculable.

As much as we would like to avert all war, most of us accept the grim fact that sometimes it is inescapable. There comes a time when diplomacy, offers, and counteroffers inevitably break down. There comes a point when a line is crossed from which there can be no return. The die is cast, and the war is on. When that time arrives, each side begins massive, all-out preparations with one goal and one goal only in mind: to win the war. Nothing less than total victory will be accepted, because a partial victory is no victory at all.

Although we all know about war and have even studied innumerable histories of wars in school, few of us apply that same knowledge to the spiritual realm of life. We live as though automatic peace, joy, and love are ours once we come to Christ. We want to live the "good life" and avoid conflict. After all, "Isn't that what Christ died for?" we reason.

Such a thought may be comforting, but it is far from the truth. Jesus Himself said, "Do not think that I came to bring peace on earth. I did not come to bring peace but a sword" (Matt. 10:34). Conflict, strife, struggle, and opposition are part of this earthly life, and denying their reality does not make it any less so. If we are going to live victoriously in Christ, we are going to have to face the fact that we are in a spiritual war as real as any natural war that has ever been fought.

That's the point of this small book you're holding in your hands. I want to teach you about the very real spiritual war that you are in. I want to teach you how to engage the enemy and come out on top. I want to teach you his tactics and the weapons you use to overcome him. I want to "teach your hands to war," as David the psalmist said. And I want you to emerge victorious over every demon in hell that tries to come between you and the God you serve. That's my purpose as we learn together God's principles of spiritual warfare.

Learning Spiritual Warfare

Psalm 18 is full of the imagery of war. David wrote it as a song of praise to God on the day when God delivered him from his enemies. The entire psalm speaks of victory in battle, and the overriding theme is the awesome power of God. It would do you well to read the psalm in its entirety, but for now, look at verses 28 through 34:

> For You will light my lamp;
> The Lord my God will enlighten my darkness.
> For by You I can run against a troop,
> By my God I can leap over a wall.
> As for God, His way is perfect;
> The word of the Lord is proven;
> He is a shield to all who trust in Him.
> For who is God, except the Lord?
> And who is a rock, except our God?
> It is God who arms me with strength,
> And makes my way perfect.
> He makes my feet like the feet of deer,
> And sets me on my high places.
> He teaches my hands to make war,
> So that my arms can bend a bow of bronze.

Verse 34 of this powerful psalm says, "He teaches my hands to make war." Notice the verb: *teaches*. That tells me that warfare is not something we automatically know how to do, but something we have to learn. God Himself will be our teacher and show us how to war in the power of the Holy Spirit. He is the one who teaches us to war.

David recognized his ignorance of warfare and total dependence upon God. He knew where his strength lay and who granted him victory in battle. Through the circumstances of his life, he learned how to war and emerge victorious against his enemies. Taught by the Master Teacher, he became a skilled warrior.

God's people as a whole are generally untrained in the art of spiritual warfare and woefully ill prepared to thwart an attack from the devil. Most of them live from day to day doing the best they can and hoping they can endure until the end and somehow make it into heaven. They possess little sense of personal victory and act more like victims of circumstance than skilled soldiers in God's army. They lack the intimate knowledge that David had of the victory that was his because of his relationship with God.

In Psalm 18, you don't find a timid, shrinking David. He's not crouching behind a bush, petrified and afraid of what Saul might do. He's bold and confident: "I can run against a troop. . . . I can leap over a wall. . . . My arms can bend a bow of bronze." He's a warrior-king who knows the source of his strength.

David spent his entire life learning how to war. He constantly battled a known enemy determined to kill him, and he had to remain vigilant against his tactics. To let down his guard for even a moment could have meant certain death. Thus David became a warrior. He may not have wanted to and he might have wished for an easier life, but the circumstances of David's life were thrust upon him, and he had no choice but to learn to fight.

Over the course of time, God sent men to assist David. The first group, however, wasn't exactly composed of the kind of men you might expect to build an army with. "And everyone who was in distress, everyone who was in debt, and everyone who was discontented gathered to him" (1 Sam. 22:2). How would you like to have a bunch like that? That's exactly what God gave David!

As David learned to war, he apparently taught his men, and over time they learned what he had learned. In fact, later in Scripture we see them described, along with others who had joined them, as David's "mighty men, helpers in the war" (1 Chron. 12:1). These men were quite skilled, "armed with bows, using both the right hand and the left in hurling stones and shooting arrows with the bow" (v. 2). In other words, they could fight the enemy from any side from which he attacked. It made no difference to them whether the assault came from the left or from the right, because they were highly skilled in the art of warfare.

In verse 8 of 1 Chronicles 12, the ranks of David's army expanded with the addition of some Gadites: "mighty men of valor, men trained for battle, who could handle shield and spear, whose faces were like the faces of lions, and were as swift as gazelles on the mountains." The lion is described as the king of the jungle, and his power is undisputed. I happen to live fairly close to a zoo, and sometimes when I am outside, I can hear the lions roar. I'm two miles away, but their roar is so powerful that it carries all the way to my house. When I hear them roar, something on the inside of me is very glad that they are contained and not prowling on the loose in my backyard!

David's mighty men oozed this kind of raw strength and brute force. They didn't have worried, furrowed brows and eyes darting to and fro to see who might attack them. They had strong faces of courage and could stand up to any foe foolish enough to attack. They were proactive, confident, self-assured warriors.

These same mighty men were also as swift as gazelles. No plodding along for them, but quick, decisive action was their trademark. Scripture describes one of David's men, Asahel, this way: "Asahel could run like a deer. . . . He was relentless and single-minded in his pursuit" (2 Sam. 2:18, 19 NLT). Nothing could stop Asahel from the task at hand, even when it meant death (v. 23). That's how determined he was.

God wants to number you in His mighty men. He wants to see you running against a troop and leaping over walls. He wants to build you up so that you can be a victorious warrior in His army. He wants to teach your hands to war.

Age is irrelevant. I don't care if you're eighteen, forty-eight, or eighty-eight; the Lord wants you to throw your shoulders back, open your mouth wide, and let out a roar that will be heard two miles away. He wants you to be a mighty man or woman of valor, and He wants to hear you bellow with the voice of victory.

Four Areas of Training in Spiritual Warfare

God's people are generally untrained in spiritual warfare. Many reasons exist that could account for this, but there are four primary areas, I think, that must be addressed in order to explain this tendency. If we can understand these areas and how they influence our ability to fight against the devil, then we can rise to the challenge of becoming mighty soldiers in the army of God.

Awareness

The first reason people are untrained in spiritual warfare is that they don't even recognize that a war is raging. In other words, they are oblivious to the fact that a spiritual battle is taking place every day on the playing field of their lives. They are one-dimensional, seeing and believing only what they can experience through their physical senses or intellects.

That is an entirely all too common scenario in most of our churches. So many people attend church week after week, sitting in the same pews around the same people listening to the same sermons, but never comprehending that they have a very real enemy who wants nothing more than to utterly destroy them. These people don't have the slightest idea what demons are or that they even exist. They are altogether unaware of this aspect of the spiritual realm.

One of the biggest lies the devil has ever circulated is that he doesn't exist. If he can get you to believe that he is only some medieval concept of evil and not a real entity, then he will have free rein in your life. If you don't believe he exists, then, of course, you don't believe that he can harm you, and you certainly don't believe that you need to resist him. Blind to his reality, you become an easy target for him and his demons.

The truth is, however, that Satan and demons are very real. Scriptures abound with accounts of their evil acts. If Satan is not real, then Jesus must be a liar because He spent approximately one-third of his ministry casting demons out of people and taking authority over them. Furthermore, when Jesus encountered demons, He spoke to them and addressed them, just like He did with people. Finally, when Jesus was tempted in the wilderness, a very real devil appeared to Him, talked with Him, and tried to do everything within his power to cause Him to sin. So when I talk about Satan or his demons, I'm not talking about some principle of evil, some vague force that's in all of us. I'm talking about a *person,* a totally evil person who wants to annihilate you and me.

When people don't know that they are in a war against a very real devil, their behavior reflects that lack of knowledge. They realize that something is wrong in their lives, but they can't quite figure out what it is. They think that they must have bad luck or that people are out to get them or that they're just going through a bad time, but they never really quite grasp the true nature of their struggles.

It's similar to what a former pastor at Bethany said one time. He related a fictitious story about a boxer who didn't know the source of the blows he was suffering. Unable to figure out where the blows were coming from, he told his coach, "Keep your eye on the referee!"

That's the way a lot of people are. They don't know where the devil is or what he's doing to them. All they know is that they keep getting hit, and they keep blaming the wrong person.

Accuracy

A second area of spiritual warfare we need to address is accuracy. By accuracy I mean the ability to discern spirits, to know when the devil is talking to you and trying to incite you. This phase of spiritual warfare also encompasses recognizing that people are not your enemy—the devil is.

This is a critical fact to understand because most people are totally inaccurate in their assessment of who is responsible for their problems. They think Aunt Myrtle is the cause of all the turmoil at every family gathering, or they blame their stubborn spouse whenever something goes wrong. They spend their time psychologically dissecting everybody, trying to gain the upper hand and trying to figure out what everyone else is thinking. Like Pogo in the famous cartoon strip, they have concluded, "We have met the enemy and he is us!"

No, the enemy is not "us," but a real devil that wants to put a wedge between you and those you live and work with. Regardless of the battle raging between you and another person, you must recognize that he is not your enemy—the devil is. The New Testament states this very clearly: "For we are not fighting against people made of flesh and blood, but against the evil rulers and authorities of the unseen world, against those mighty powers of darkness who rule this world, and against wicked spirits in the heavenly realms" (Eph. 6:12 NLT).

"But," you protest, "my neighbor is suing me. Surely that makes him my enemy." Or maybe you think, "My husband is so ornery I *know* he's my enemy." No, your neighbor is not your enemy, and neither is your husband. No person on the face of the earth is your enemy. The problem is, you're looking at the person who seems to be causing you grief without discerning below the surface as to who is motivating and influencing him.

In guerrilla warfare, it is almost impossible to recognize the enemy because he looks and acts just like everyone else. He goes about his business for a while, but then all of a sudden, he springs and launches his attack. That's the way the devil operates. He bobs and weaves, jumps and ducks; he hides and disguises himself. He talks through people and uses them to push your buttons, and before you know it, you're fighting everybody but the devil. You're letting loose with both barrels, but the only problem is, you're shooting at the wrong target. You need accuracy.

Artillery

The third reason that people don't engage in spiritual warfare is ignorance of the authority and spiritual weapons they can use against the devil. Because no one has taught them about spiritual authority, they assume they are defenseless against the devil's schemes. They are afraid to enter into any battle against a foe they think is stronger than they are.

The bulk of the Christian world, I think, fits into this category. They acknowledge the existence of a very real devil and even recognize when he is attacking them, but they don't know how to use the weapons they have at their disposal. They just hope for the best as they slog along in life. Their goal is to endure until the end and make it into heaven, even if it's just by the skin of their teeth.

Many of these people have made a compromise with the devil: "You leave me alone, and I'll leave you alone." They hope by lying low they can avoid confrontation with him. The devil, however, doesn't play that game. He's thrilled if you want to leave him alone, but he will *never* leave you alone. His intent is clear—to steal, kill, and destroy—and he exempts no one from his evil plans.

You have a choice. Either you can learn to fight the devil, or you can get whipped. You can use the authority and weapons God has given you, or you can just lie down and become the devil's doormat. Those really are the only two options.

It's imperative to understand that Jesus' death on the cross not only won your salvation but totally destroyed the devil's power. He is already a vanquished foe! He knows he's been defeated; he just hopes you don't find out.

Sir Francis Bacon (1561–1626) said, "Knowledge is power," and in the spiritual realm, that is particularly true. You don't whimper and hide from something that has no power to harm you. Once you know that the bee lacks a stinger, you're not afraid of it; once you know the snake has no fangs, you don't fear it. And once you know the devil has already been defeated, you're not afraid of him either.

The Lord wants to give you boldness in place of fear. He wants you to walk in the supernatural authority and power He has given you. He stated this quite distinctly to His disciples: "Behold, I give you the authority to trample on serpents and scorpions, and over all the power of the enemy, and nothing shall by any means hurt you" (Luke 10:19). Jesus has taken the teeth out of the snake, and he can't hurt you anymore. You don't have to be afraid that the snake will lash out and inject his venom into you, because Jesus has already crushed his head (Gen. 3:15), and you can trample on the rest of him!

Believers who know their spiritual authority are not afraid of the devil. They don't go out looking to engage him, but when he rears his head against them (as he is sure to do), they don't hesitate to swiftly bring their foot down upon him. They unleash their artillery and let him have it. They call on the blood of Jesus, they loose His powerful name, they stand on the Word of God, and they worship in the midst of the fight. They're warriors, bold and fearless in the day of battle.

Active Duty

A fourth category of people concerning spiritual warfare are those who refuse to go on active duty. They are aware of the devil's existence, recognize him as their enemy, and are familiar with all the weapons and authority they can use against him. There's just one problem: They never actually get around to rising up and fighting him!

It would do a soldier no good to know all about the enemy and be trained in the use of all manner of weapons if all he did was stay in the barracks and sleep. The enemy would soon make quick work of him. Yet that's just how some Christians act. They sit in church Sunday after Sunday, taking voluminous notes on spiritual warfare and amening every Scripture verse the pastor throws out, but when Monday rolls around and the devil attacks, they just sit there like a bump on a log. They don't stand toe-to-toe with the devil and order him out of their lives. Refusing to exert the energy it would take to run him off, they tolerate him a little here and a little there until he has encroached quite a bit more than they ever intended.

There is not one ounce of goodness or mercy in the devil, so you can't afford to allow him even an inch in your life. Peter knew this; that's why he instructed us to "be sober, be vigilant; because your adversary the devil walks about like a roaring lion, seeking whom he may devour" (1 Pet. 5:8). The word *vigilant* means three things. It means to be on guard against something, to not tolerate it, and to be zealously active against it. In spiritual warfare, it means to be sober, wary, and proactive. It never means sitting back with a "Qué será, será" attitude.

An unfortunate thing about humans, however, is that we don't like to confront things or expend too much energy against something. We see this in the children of Israel after they went into Canaan. God had promised them this land, but they still had to go in and possess it. They had to actively participate in the process in order to enjoy their full inheritance, and that's just what they did at first.

As Joshua 10 records, they went in and began conquering cities: Jericho, Ai, and Jerusalem, to name a few. They killed five kings, won battle after battle, and even witnessed

Joshua's stopping the sun at Gibeon. They were marching toward everything God had promised them and enjoying great success. Somewhere along the way, however, some of the tribes grew complacent. They became satisfied with where they were and really didn't want to continue fighting.

That, however, was not God's plan for them. Joshua addressed the people of Israel and encouraged them to press forward for all that God had for them. He said, "How long are ye slack to go to possess the land, which the Lord God of your fathers hath given you?" (Josh. 18:3 KJV). He addressed their spiritual laziness, and that's what it is when you refuse to engage the enemy, when you're content with the land of "good enough" and don't want to fight for all that God has for you.

I know what some of you are thinking: "Well, I'm doing pretty good. I've got no complaints. Thank God, I'm saved, filled with the Holy Spirit, and on my way to heaven. I know I don't see much victory in some areas, but I can get by without that. I'm doing all right just like I am." No, you're not doing all right, and the devil will find that one chink in your armor and go in for the kill.

You'd better be vigilant about possessing whatever spiritual land you've been lacking. If it's healing, then start exercising your faith in that area. Go on the offensive. Every day verbally assert your victory and let the devil know you're in charge. Keep advancing against him until he has no choice but to retreat.

You can never relax your guard against the devil, even after you've experienced a great victory. Some people fight a horrendous battle against the devil and persevere until they win, but then they let their guard down because they think he's never going to return again. That's not what the Scriptures say. "When an unclean spirit goes out of a man, he goes through dry places, seeking rest; and finding none, he says, 'I will return to my house from which I came' " (Luke

11:24). You can count on a counterattack from the devil any time you experience even a little bit of victory. The trick is, don't be surprised by it, and don't think you won't be tested in some other area as well.

You can never rest on your laurels in spiritual warfare. You can never stop being ruthless in your dealings with the devil. You can never afford to grow lazy and sloppy and let the devil do just whatever he wants in your life. You've got to get downright vicious in your resistance to him and unwavering in your determination to remain vigilant. You've got to be on active duty in the army of God and not go spiritually AWOL.

A man in our church discovered what happens when you move from inactive to active duty. For five years, he had remained on inactive duty, as far as physical health goes. He had arthritis and for a long time simply tolerated it. You know how it is. You think, "Well, I'm getting old. It's not so bad. My mother had arthritis, and I guess it just runs in my family." That's how this man thought until one day he had had enough. He moved from inactive duty to active duty. He picked up his spiritual weapons and began using his authority. He made a list of fifteen Scriptures that dealt with healing and began reading and meditating on them daily. Every day he served notice on the devil and claimed his healing. After three weeks, the stiffness and swelling of arthritis left his body for the first time in five years. But it didn't happen until he became active in spiritual warfare.

I love Smith Wigglesworth's illustration of what happens when we use our spiritual authority. He once related a story about a woman at a bus stop who was threatened by a little dog. This little dog approached her, barking for all he was worth, and she froze in place as she timidly said, "Go on back now; go on." The dog did not retreat, so she repeated her plea: "Go on back now; go on." The bus approached and she had to get on it, so with much fear she turned to the dog, stomped her foot, and firmly said, "Scat!" With that the dog turned around, put his tail between his legs, and took off running.

That's exactly how it is with the devil. He barks and lunges and bares his teeth, but the moment you pick up your spiritual weapons and yell "Scat!" he turns tail and runs. You don't have to tolerate him for a minute. Don't put up with a little bit of his activity here or a little bad habit there. If you invite him in for a minute, he'll want to stay forever, and that little thing you tolerated will turn into a terrible bondage.

Don't tolerate *anything* from the devil. If someone offends you, don't take the devil's bait and start thinking about how that person has wronged you. Don't listen to his accusations against the person. If God has been dealing with you about objectionable books or objects in your house, ignore the devil's whispers that it's really no big deal. Be absolutely ruthless against him. No matter what, recognize his attacks, pull out your spiritual artillery, and use every weapon at your disposal. That's how you wage spiritual warfare, and that's how you find victory.

The Need to War

If you stop and think about it, God could vanquish all our enemies with one fell swoop. One puff of His breath, one flick of His finger could wipe the devil off the face of the earth forever. Yet he allows him rein, at least for a season, and there's a reason for that. In Judges 3:1–2 NIV, the Bible says, "These are the nations the Lord left to test all those Israelites who had not experienced any of the wars in Canaan (he did this only *to teach warfare* to the descendants of the Israelites who had not had previous battle experience)" (emphasis added). Then the passage goes on to list the names of the peoples that still inhabited Israel's Promised Land.

Isn't it interesting that after the first generation of Israelites entered Canaan, an entirely new generation arose that had never experienced warfare and God's mighty saving power? The Word of God says that God had to teach them warfare, just like He had taught their predecessors. They couldn't ride on the coattails of their fathers all their lives. There came a time when God said *they* had to learn for themselves how to war against their enemies.

Each one of us has got to learn how to fight our own spiritual battles. No one can do it for us. *You* have to know you have a real enemy; *you* have to discern his working; *you* have to take out your spiritual artillery; and *you* have to rise up and fight him.

Some of you know that but have grown discouraged because you've been defeated in a battle or two already. You say, "Pastor, I've tried all that, but it didn't work for me." Well, God is going to lift up your gloves again. He's going to "strengthen the hands which hang down, and the feeble knees, and make straight paths for your feet" (Heb. 12:12, 13). I like it even better the way the NLT says it: "So take a new grip with your tired hands and stand firm on your shaky legs. Mark out a straight path for your feet." Yes, you're tired, and yes, your legs are shaking, but get up one more time and go out swinging for all you're worth. The Lord is fighting for you!

I've made up my mind that I'm not going spiritually AWOL. I refuse to give the devil one inch in my life or in my family. He may win a battle or two, but I'm going to win the war. When he comes against me, he's going to know he's in the ring with somebody. I might get my ears boxed and my nose broken, but I'm going to keep on punching. I'm going to keep letting God guide my hands, teaching me to war.

The Real War: Whom Will You Worship?

I keep saying we're in a war, but what exactly is this war all about? To answer that question, we have to go back to the time when Satan was cast out of heaven. Satan, or Lucifer as he was called, wanted to be exalted. Perhaps his position in leading worship in heaven went to his head, but regardless of the cause, he led a rebellion against God with one-third of the angels. He was swiftly punished and banished from heaven, along with the fallen angels. Following his fall, he showed up on the earth.

God created human beings to worship Him by choice and because of love. Only to them did God give the capability of worshiping Him as Creator. Animals can't do that, and neither can plants nor inanimate objects; that is something reserved to humans alone. Thus with the creation of human beings, the stage was set for spiritual war. On one side was Lucifer, whose sole plan was to degrade humanity and steal their worship of God. On the other side was the supreme God over all, the only one worthy of all true worship. Humanity was placed right in the middle of this situation. Human beings had to choose whom they would worship: God or Satan.

That's what the entire course of human history is all about. "Choose you this day whom ye will serve," challenged Joshua (Josh. 24:15 KJV). Each person must answer for himself and, hopefully, like Joshua respond, "As for me and my house, we will serve the Lord." The central question of all time is "Whom will you worship, and whom will you serve?" That question is the reason there is an ongoing war for the souls of humankind.

Even Jesus had to answer this fundamental question of worship. When Satan tempted Him in the wilderness, he blatantly tried to get Jesus to worship him. He tried to make a deal with Jesus. "If you'll worship me, I'll give you everything," he offered. Jesus, of course, was not about to worship the devil, and Scripture records His answer: "Away with you, Satan! For it is written, 'You shall worship the Lord your God, and Him only you shall serve'" (Matt. 4:10).

Story after story in the Bible repeats this ongoing war over worship. Perhaps the best known story of all is the story of Job in the Old Testament. The very first chapter of this book in the Bible makes it quite clear that the issue at hand concerned Job's choice of whom he would worship and serve. In verse 8, God spoke and said to Satan, "Have you considered My servant Job, that there is none like him on the earth, a blameless and upright man, one who fears God and shuns evil?" Isn't it wonderful the way God bragged on Job? He called him upright and blameless and identified him as a God-fearing man.

Satan, though, had a ready answer. In effect, he told God, "Well, that may be true, but the only reason Job worships You is because You've put a hedge around him and blessed him. If You took away everything dear to him, he'd forget about You in a hurry!"

"All right, you may test him," the Lord said to Satan. "Do whatever you want with everything he possesses, but don't harm him physically" (v. 12 NLT). The next ten verses record all the evil things the devil did to try to get Job to turn his back on the God he had worshiped all his life. It's very clear from these verses that it was the devil—not God—who did these things.

Job's reaction to the multiple catastrophes that hit him in one day is absolutely astounding. He had to choose whether or not he was still going to serve God, despite the horrific circumstances that had come his way. Look what he did: "Then Job arose, tore his robe, and shaved his head; and he fell to the ground and *worshiped*. And he said: 'Naked I came from my mother's womb, and naked shall I return there. The Lord gave, and the Lord has taken away; blessed be the name of the Lord' " (vv. 20–21, emphasis added). In the midst of the most unimaginable horror of losing his children, workers, possessions, and material wealth, Job worshiped.

Satan lost that battle when Job worshiped, and God was proven right in His assessment of Job's unswerving devotion to Him. Job was right in the middle of a spiritual war, and both God and Satan watched to see the course of action he would choose. Without missing a beat, Job chose to worship God, and even when his circumstances deteriorated further, he kept choosing to worship God.

Just like Job, you are on spiritual display. There is a theater of war, and you are the leading actor. All eyes are upon you. The devil is betting that you won't worship God if your life takes a turn for the worse, but God is bragging on you: "Have you seen my servant Dan or Stephen or Jason (or any other name)? There is no one like him. He'll never turn from me, because his heart is blameless." He has so much confidence in you that He'll allow Satan to attack just to prove your devotion.

Satan doesn't know it, but he's the most used being in the universe. God's got him on a leash. Yes, Satan attacks, but he can go no farther than the reach of that leash. He can lunge and pull and snarl all he wants, but God is the one holding the leash. He's waiting to see what you are made of in the heat of trial. He's waiting to see whom you will worship.

No matter how hot the battle gets or how the trials pile up, God will never leave you alone to slug it out with the devil. First Corinthians 10:13 says, "No temptation has overtaken you except such as is common to man; but God is faithful, who will not allow you to be tempted beyond what you are able, but with the temptation will also make the way of escape, that you may be able to bear it." You've got that promise to see you through any trial, temptation, or calamity the devil throws your way.

Just like God did with the Israelites, He'll leave a few enemies in your land that He'll use to teach you how to war. That's their purpose in your life. You'll find out your true mettle, and you'll learn how to pick up your spiritual weapons and fight, after you've been attacked a few times. God, of course, knows the outcome of every battle you'll face, but He wants you to see yourself as you really are, and He wants you to reaffirm your choice to worship Him.

When you are tempted to grow weary in the battles of life, remember that warfare is only temporary, but worship is eternal. There will be no warfare in heaven and no weapons of any kind. Worship will be the order of the day, and the devil won't be anywhere around. Do you realize that for most of your existence, the devil will play absolutely no role in your life? He won't be able to interject a depressing thought. Worry will never plague you again. You'll have no desire for a cigarette. You'll live in health, wealth, and joy in a place that Jesus has been preparing for you for over two thousand years.

As wonderful as all that is and as surely as it is your ultimate destiny, right now on this earth, you are in the theater of war. Through the things He allows in your life, God is teaching you to war. James 1:2–3 NLT says, "Whenever trouble comes your way, let it be an opportunity for joy. For when your faith is tested, your endurance has a chance to grow."

Some of you have been trying to figure out why you are battling so many things. Take courage from the Scriptures. Your trials are your friends, come to test your faith and prove your allegiance to God. The devil is watching ever so closely to see what you are going to do. Why don't you just lift your hands and worship? Why don't you just shout hallelujah? Why don't you lift up your head to heaven, throw your head back, and laugh to your heart's content? Why don't you choose to worship?

The Real Enemy: Satan

Some people don't even know there's a war on, but then others just don't know who their enemy is. We touched on this a little bit already, but I want to look at it in more detail.

Your enemy is never a person, though it can sure seem that way. Because Satan and his forces are disembodied spirits, they seek to inhabit people in order to express themselves. They look for physical bodies that they can inhabit and use for their vile purposes.

Demonic forces seek influence in several ways (this is covered in more detail in chapter 6). The primary way they try to influence is through the human thought process. This involves an interjection of a voice that speaks to the human mind. If you have a thought that just pops into your mind, especially if it does not line up with the Word of God, that's a pretty good indication that it is a demonic thought, or "high thought," as it is sometimes called. This kind of thought whispers rebellion, violence, hatred, and impurity. It seems to come from nowhere.

If you entertain such a thought often enough, it becomes entrenched in your mind. It gradually infiltrates your being until you have embraced the thought to such an extent that you can no longer differentiate it from yourself. You view the thought as truth and become motivated by suspicion. You blame others for your problems because you don't recognize the source of all the thoughts running through your mind.

Jesus always recognized the enemy. He never failed to understand that flesh and blood was not his enemy, but Satan himself. In Matthew 16, Jesus began telling His disciples about what lay ahead for Him. He talked about His impending suffering and how it would culminate in His death. He was trying to prepare His disciples for what was coming, but Peter couldn't receive it. I'm sure a high thought entered his mind, or else he would never have dared do what he did in verse 22: "But Peter took him aside and corrected him. 'Heaven forbid, Lord,' he said. 'This will never happen to you!' " (NLT).

Can you imagine the nerve of anyone who would correct the Lord? But that's exactly what Peter did. Because what

Jesus spoke was so repugnant to him, Peter could not believe that it was so. I believe a thought entered his mind, a little voice that said, "No, that's not right." And before he had even thought about it, it exploded into his consciousness and out of his mouth.

That thought did not come from Peter. We have no record that he had ever spoken so irreverently before, but better proof is found in Jesus' answer to him. "Jesus turned to Peter and said, 'Get away from me, Satan! You are a dangerous trap to me. You are seeing things merely from a human point of view, and not from God's' " (v. 23 NLT). Jesus recognized that Peter had yielded to a thought implanted in his mind and had blurted it out. Thus Jesus did not rebuke the man Peter, but the spirit who spoke out of him. He knew His enemy.

This is a vital part of spiritual warfare: knowing who the enemy is and discerning when he is using another person's speech, thoughts, or actions to come against you. If you are a Christian, Satan loves nothing more than to stir up people against you. But you've got to recognize his tactics. That way you won't get mad at the person on the job who seems to dislike you and is trying to sabotage your promotion. You won't start circulating stories about him or try to explain yourself to everyone. You'll choose to worship God because you know who the real enemy is.

The Primary Weapon: Worship

The mightiest weapon in spiritual warfare is worship. Since worship is also the crux of the war, it makes sense that a determination to praise and worship God in the middle of the war would be our most powerful weapon. We know, of course, that we can use the blood of Jesus, His name, and the Word of God as weapons. Much has been written on these topics, and you've probably read any number of books about how to use them. Worship, however, is often an overlooked topic, as far as spiritual warfare goes.

Back in the first three verses of Psalm 18, we see this key of worship as a weapon of deliverance:

> I will love You, O Lord, my strength.
> The Lord is my rock and my fortress and my deliverer;
> My God, my strength, in whom I will trust;
> My shield and the horn of my salvation, my stronghold.
> I will call upon the Lord, who is worthy to be praised;
> So shall I be saved from my enemies.

Although this is a prophetic psalm about the Lord Jesus Christ, its principles apply to believers as well. In the first three verses, the psalmist proclaims his faith in God as deliverer. Verse 3 holds the key as to how his deliverance will come: "I will call upon the Lord, who is worthy to be praised" (worship) / "So shall I be saved from my enemies" (deliverance). When the believer cries out to God for help and lifts his voice in worship, God hears and moves mightily, and when God begins moving, look what happens (v. 7):

> Then the earth shook and trembled;
> The foundations of the hills also quaked and were shaken,
> Because He was angry.

When God is on your side, nothing can stop your deliverance; no obstacle can prevent Him from coming to your aid. Psalm 18:9–10 says it so descriptively:

> He bowed the heavens also, and came down
> With darkness under His feet.
> And He rode upon a cherub, and flew;
> He flew upon the wings of the wind.

Can't you just see it? The God of the universe, opening the heavens and riding on a cherub, *flying* to your defense! Never let the devil tell you God doesn't care, that He's taking too long to help you. God *flies* to your defense!

The psalm continues in verses 13 and 14:

> The Lord thundered from heaven,
> And the Most High uttered His voice,
> Hailstones and coals of fire.
> He sent out His arrows and scattered the foe,
> Lightnings in abundance, and He vanquished them.

Did you know that God can send hailstones on the enemy, shoot arrows at the wicked, and totally destroy every scheme of the devil? He doesn't just contain the devil—He vanquishes him! That means total victory and complete domination, not partial or incomplete.

God's mighty power is released when we worship. He moves heaven and earth to rescue those who choose to worship Him. He vanquishes every foe and pulls out all the stops to come to the aid of the one who has chosen to worship. That's how powerful a weapon is worship, and we are going to study it in detail.

Chapter 2

Worship As a Weapon and Hindrances to Fighting

In the last chapter, I identified worship as your primary weapon in warfare. It is so critical to your ability to successfully fight the enemy that I'm going to devote the first part of this chapter to it. The devil does not want you to praise and worship God. More than anything else, he makes it his mission to steal your worship of God. That's what he tried to do before the beginning of time, and that's what he still attempts to do today. Desiring the worship that belongs to God alone, he is constantly vying for your worship. He knows if he can get you to worship him even in a subtle way or if he can keep you from worshiping God, then he can defeat you.

At any given time, the most powerful weapon you have at your disposal is your ability to lift your hands and worship God for saving you and delivering you from the snare of the enemy. When you do that, you visibly demonstrate that you have turned your back on the devil and turned to God. In that moment, you unleash the power of God to intervene on your behalf.

Unfortunately, we don't always do that. If you're like me, the first thing that happens when you're attacked is that you start feeling sorry for yourself. "Poor me. Why does everything bad happen to me?" you think. As much as you might enjoy thinking like that, self-pity is a faith-killer and plays right into the devil's hands. You might feel sorry for yourself and manage to get everyone else to feel sorry for you too, but the devil is not going to join in and say, "Poor thing, you're right. You've suffered enough; I believe I'll just leave you alone."

The devil has no mercy. He is totally evil, and all his thoughts toward you are designed to steal, kill, or destroy. He's like a poisonous snake, coiled and waiting to strike. Get it in your spirit that the devil *hates* you. He is your sworn enemy, and that fact will never change.

You have one choice and one choice only—if you want to be victorious—when the devil strikes. No matter how you feel, rise up and actively resist him. Like Esther dare to say, "If I perish, I perish, but I'm going to worship the king" (Esther 4:16). Set your face like a flint, and be resolute in your determination to keep your focus on the God you worship. When you do that, you remove yourself from the dominion of the devil and plant yourself squarely in the kingdom of God.

Worship As a Weapon

David understood this connection between worship and warfare. In Psalm 144:1 KJV, he said, "Blessed be the Lord my strength, which teacheth my hands to war, and my fingers to fight." David wasn't going around looking for a fight; he wasn't talking about bullying people "in the name of the Lord." There was no arrogance in David, but experience had taught him that God was on his side and would teach him how to defeat every enemy that came against him.

In verse 2 of Psalm 144 KJV, David extolled God's character: "My goodness, and my fortress; my high tower and my deliverer; my shield, and he in whom I trust." David knew who God was and was secure in that. Notice also how he chose military terms in describing God's power: "fortress," "tower," "deliverer," "shield." He knew the intimate connection between praising God and warring in His strength.

David was a shepherd before he was ever a soldier. He had not been raised in an atmosphere of battle, and his father was not a military general. David's upbringing had taught him nothing about warfare. All David knew how to do was to take care of sheep, a solitary occupation. It did not require a lot of activity on David's part; he carried a harp, not a harpoon. In his role as a shepherd, he didn't have to wear armor or arm himself with weapons each day. While his brothers were off with Saul fighting against Israel's enemies, David was in the field, strumming his harp and singing the songs God had placed in his heart. Day after day and through the evening hours, that young man learned to worship.

An interesting thing happened as David the shepherd boy worshiped. He discovered that when a lion or bear appeared to attack the sheep, he could take care of it. He told Saul about this in 1 Samuel 17:34–35: "Your servant used to keep his father's sheep, and when a lion or a bear came and took a lamb out of the flock, I went out after it and struck it, and delivered the lamb from its mouth; and when it arose against me, I caught it by its beard, and struck and killed it." The boy who had spent his days singing and strumming a harp rose up like a fierce warrior when an enemy threatened his sheep. All those days spent worshiping had deposited iron in his soul and transformed him into a mighty man of battle.

David and Goliath

The day came when David's skill as a bold, fearless warrior was revealed to all Israel. The story in 1 Samuel 17 is probably one of the most well-known and well-loved stories in the Bible. David's father sent him to the battlefield to bring provisions to his brothers, who were fighting with Saul. Obediently David went and arrived just in time to hear Goliath taunting the armies of Israel. Something stirred on the inside of David at that moment, I believe. The anointing that he carried upon him from all the hours spent worshiping rose up, and the little shepherd boy indignantly proclaimed, "Who is this uncircumcised Philistine, that he should defy the armies of the living God?" (v. 26).

This thing just came over David. "How dare anyone insult my God!" he thought. "I'll take him on, and the same God that enabled me to kill the lion and the bear will help me kill this uncircumcised Philistine." So the seventeen-year-old boy rose up like a tiger to take on the fearsome, dreaded Philistine who had struck terror in the hearts of the entire army of Israel.

Not everyone was impressed with David's bold statements, however. His own brother, Eliab, accused him of pride and insolence. Look how he derided him: "Why did you come down here? And with whom have you left *those few sheep* in the wilderness?" (v. 28, emphasis added). In other words, he was saying, "Who do you think you are, David? Go on back to those little old sheep you're taking care of. That's all you're good for." There will always be those who try to keep you from going to battle, but like David, you can't listen to them.

David, undeterred by his brother's contempt, was brought before King Saul, where he again stated his intention of taking on Goliath. Saul agreed to the plan but told David to wear his armor for protection. I can just see it. David put on Saul's helmet, and it hung past his shoulders. He put on the breastplate, and it hung to the knees. He buckled on the sword, and it dragged on the ground. Finally, he had had enough. "That's not the way I fight," he insisted. "I'm not used to such things. Let me do it my way, and the God who delivered me from the lion and the bear will deliver me from this Philistine."

You know the end of the story. "He picked up five smooth stones from a stream and put them in his shepherd's bag. Then, armed only with his shepherd's staff and sling, he started across to fight Goliath" (v. 40 NIV). All David knew was how to be a shepherd, so he used the tools he was familiar with.

The Scriptures don't say this, but I imagine David went out singing in worship as he advanced against Goliath. That's what he always did. And as he drew near the Philistine, he practically roared across the distance:

"You come to me with a sword, with a spear, and with a javelin. But I come to you in the name of the Lord of hosts, the God of the armies of Israel, whom you have defied. This day the Lord will deliver you into my hand, and I will strike you and take your head from you. And this day I will give the carcasses of the camp of the Philistines to the birds of the air and the wild beasts of the earth, that all the earth may know that there is a God in Israel" (vv. 45–46).

Have you ever heard such daring, such brash courage? There was no doubt in David's mind as to who would win this contest. His days of worship had convinced him of God's integrity and power, and he knew who went into battle with him. Armed with only a slingshot and five stones, the teenaged boy prevailed against mighty Goliath.

The Power in Praise

Praise is an awesome thing. It is not something we do in a prescribed manner or at a specific time of day. It is not a list of rules to follow or certain songs to sing. Praise is the lifestyle of a heart totally surrendered to God, and praise involves every aspect of the worshiper's body, mind, and spirit.

Psalm 149 tells us some of the ways we can praise the Lord and when we can praise Him. Verse 1 instructs us to "sing in the assembly of saints." Verse 3 says to praise Him "with the dance" and "with timbrel [tambourine] and harp." Verse 5 is interesting:

> Let the saints be joyful in glory;
> Let them sing aloud on their beds.

And verse 6 says, "Let the high praises of God be *in their mouth*" (emphasis added). Where are the praises? In their mouths! Not in their minds or their hearts or in their thoughts, but in their mouths! That means it's to be verbal, spoken aloud, shouted from the rooftops. Some of you say, "Oh, I praise God in my heart. I don't believe in all that loud stuff." Well, it's fine to praise Him in your heart, but you've got to let the praise come out of your mouth too.

What if you walked around your house day after day and thought about how wonderful your husband or wife was and even gazed lovingly at him or her but never opened your mouth to say "I love you"? Do you think that would suffice in your relationship with your spouse? Of course not! Love is meant to be verbally expressed, and it's no different in your relationship with God.

The second part of verse 6 in Psalm 149 says you have to not only have God's praises in your mouth, but you also have to have a two-edged sword in your hand. Once more the correlation and interrelationship between worship and warfare are obvious. We praise, and then we fight; we worship, and then we war.

Worship should always precede warfare because worship provides the ability to war effectively. That means that when the trials accumulate in your life and the heat is turned high, you've got to turn up your praise and worship of God. Praise Him for all He is worth and with everything within you, and watch how much more effective your warfare becomes. The two are inseparable.

David and Ziklag

David was intimately acquainted with the connection between worship and warfare. In Psalm 47:1–3, he wrote:

Oh, clap your hands, all you peoples!
Shout to God with the voice of triumph!
For the Lord Most High is awesome;
He is a great King over all the earth.
He will subdue the peoples under us,
And the nations under our feet.

Once again, worship—clapping, shouting, and extolling God—is followed by God's delivering power.

David also knew that he had to worship God at all times, regardless of circumstances. First Samuel 30 tells of a tragic circumstance that David faced that must have been almost unbearable. This tragedy occurred prior to David's becoming king; it happened during the time when he was fleeing from Saul. During that time, David had been in the land of the Philistines, and they had given him a city called Ziklag.

On the day of the tragedy, David and his men were not in Ziklag, and while they were gone, the Amalekites burned the city to the ground. As bad as that was, it got worse. The Amalekites carried off all the women and children of the city, so when David and his men returned home, they came face to face with their city destroyed and their loved ones taken captive.

I don't think most of us can even imagine what that must have been like. In America, we are so used to the protection of our local police forces and national armed forces that we just take law and order for granted. We cannot imagine what it would be like to live in a hostile area with violent, warring tribes a daily threat. But that was the reality of David's world.

David and his men were grief-stricken when they came home to their devastated city. As might be expected, "they wept until they could weep no more" (v. 4 NLT). Heartbroken, these mighty men cried until they had no more tears to shed. You know what that's like. Some of you may be there right now — decimated, overwhelmed, carrying a burden so great that you feel crushed under its weight. The questions, like an unending tape, run through your mind: "How did this happen to me? How did things go so wrong? What am I going to do?" That's how David felt.

Just when he thought his situation couldn't possibly get any worse, it did. The same men who had fought alongside him suddenly turned on him with a vengeance. "David was now in serious trouble because his men were very bitter about losing their wives and children, and they began to talk of stoning him" (v. 6a NLT). Isn't it something the way people will turn on you? Here were David's mighty men, happy and shouting as they returned home, but when tragedy hit, they turned on David like injured animals.

What do you do when your trusted friends or family members turn on you? Do you defensively "put up your dukes"? Do you run away with your tail between your legs, licking your wounds and looking for a safe place to hide? David did neither. Instead, "David strengthened himself in the Lord his God" (v. 6b NLT).

The way he did it was the same way he had done it for all his years of following God. "Bring me the ephod!" he ordered (v. 7 NLT). That is significant because the ephod was the priestly garment and symbolic of the presence of

God. When David asked for the ephod, he was signifying His decision to commune with God in worship and receive direction. David put on that ephod, received the direction he needed, and got back everything the enemy had taken. "So David recovered all that the Amalekites had carried away, and David rescued his two wives. And nothing of theirs was lacking, either small or great, sons or daughters, spoil or anything which they had taken from them; David recovered all" (vv. 18–19).

Probably nothing as tragic as what happened to David at Ziklag will ever happen to you. Nevertheless, you will face attacks. It happens to everyone, even to Spirit-filled Christians who love God and know His Word. Bad things do happen to good people.

If you're like me, every now and then you'll be walking along praising God when all of a sudden—whop! You don't know where it came from or why, but the devil suddenly throws a punch at you. You can do one of two things: You can either get mad at God and everyone else, or you can refuse to give the devil even a moment's glory in the situation. You can say, "Bring me the ephod!" or you can say, "Woe is me!" You can worship and war, or complain and give up. It's up to you.

The Relationship Between Worship and Warfare

When you resist the enemy and put on your priestly garment of praise and worship, God's power begins mobilizing on your behalf, and His anointing to break every yoke appears on the scene. If you don't stop worshiping the Lord, you'll keep your joy, even in the most difficult circumstances. As you continue in worship, God goes to battle for you and brings the victory. This is the relationship between worship and warfare.

After the Israelites miraculously crossed through the Red Sea, they faced a new battle when the Amalekites attacked. Moses, however, knew what to do, and he went up the mountain and lifted his hands in worship. As long as his hands were lifted, Israel won the battle. When he grew weary and lowered his hands, the Amalekites began winning.

In the heat of the battle, Aaron and Hur came alongside to prop up Moses' arms. They just stood there and helped hold up his hands in worship, and by the end of the day, the enemy had been thoroughly defeated. That says to me that as long as you worship, God is moving on your behalf. His forces are mobilized for you, and God's authority and anointing are upon you as you continue to worship.

This is a principle seen over and over in the Scriptures. When Joshua faced the fortified city of Jericho, the Lord didn't instruct him to war by use of arrows or battering rams. The Lord simply told him to release the shout of worship and victory, and when Joshua did, the walls of the great city fell flat before him (Josh. 6:1–21).

When Jehoshaphat faced the Moabites and the Ammonites, he knew he was powerless. Steadfastly, however, he kept his eyes on the Lord, and the Lord instructed him to stand still while He fought the battle for him. Then the Lord told him to send out the praisers, who worshiped and gave thanks to God. As they moved out worshiping, the Lord ambushed the enemy, and the entire army was routed (2 Chron. 20:1–30).

Hindrances to Fighting

No one on the face of the earth is exempt from having to learn how to fight the devil and worship God in the midst of trials and tribulations. The quicker we accept this fact, the better off we'll be and the quicker we'll start seeing victory. Despite that truth, many people still fail to actually rise up against the devil and maintain a heart of worship when they face an attack. They remain apathetic, depressed, and hopeless. They never get around to actually standing up and resisting the enemy. There are, I believe, several reasons for this.

Personal Blessing

The first area that hinders some people from being vigilant against the devil might surprise you, but it is the area of personal blessing. Sometimes blessing can become a curse. If you don't know how to keep blessing in proper perspective, it can actually work to your detriment.

Numbers 32 records that the children of Reuben and Gad owned a large number of livestock by the time they came to Gilead. Because Gilead was ideally suited for raising livestock, they asked permission from Moses to stay where they were rather than crossing over the Jordan River with their kinsmen (v. 4).

Reuben and Gad were the first two of the tribes of Israel to actually begin possessing the enemy's land and experiencing God's blessing, and as a result, they became complacent. Instead of saying to their kinsmen, "We've got our land, but now we're going to help you get yours," they said, "We have what we want, so you just go ahead without us and fight for your land."

This was a very selfish outlook, and Moses didn't allow it, and neither can you allow self-satisfaction to lull you into a false sense of security. How easy it is when everything in your life seems to be going fine to sit down and say, "Thank you, God. I don't see an enemy in sight, and everything in my life is good. I believe I'll just settle down right here on this side of the Jordan and not fight anymore." No matter how tempting, you just can't do that.

If you are so fortunate as to have no personal battles, then go to war for others. There are people all around you who are hurting, struggling, and needing someone to hold up their hands. They need someone who can teach them to war and show them how to pull down the strongholds the devil has erected in their lives. They need *you* to step alongside them and fight the battle with them.

Moses corrected this complacent, selfish attitude in Reuben and Gad and said in Numbers 32:6 NLT, "Do you mean you want to stay back here while your brothers go across and do all the fighting?" The New Living Translation is so blunt: "Do you mean . . .?" It's as though Moses could hardly believe that Reuben and Gad would consider such a ridiculous course of action.

That's how ludicrous it is to think that you can be satisfied with your blessings while thousands around you know nothing about the God who gives such wonderful blessings. It is so important that you become a warrior for the Lord Jesus Christ, knowing how to use the weapons of spiritual warfare not just for yourself, but for others.

Past Success

The second reason that some people don't fight is related to the area of past success. This subtle enemy is illustrated in the story of Elijah in 1 Kings 19. Elijah was a man of power, well-acquainted with the ways of warfare and how to defeat God's enemies. As a great prophet, he had stopped the rain for three years, and after his contest with the prophets of Baal, he prayed and rain returned to the land. Then, with the anointing of God still upon him, he outran Ahab's chariot for twenty miles.

You would have thought that after such a mountaintop experience, Elijah would have been totally invincible. But that's not the way it was. After hearing of the slaying of Baal's prophets, the evil queen Jezebel purposed to kill Elijah and sent word of her intention. With that death warrant hanging over his head, Elijah despaired, even to the point of death. The Bible says that he "went a day's journey into the wilderness, and came and sat down under a broom tree. And he prayed that he might die, and said, 'It is enough! Now, Lord, take my life, for I am no better than my fathers!' " (v. 4).

Elijah totally crashed. The mountaintop high of the great victory evaporated, and he plunged headfirst into the valley of despair. In just one day, he went from being the man of God full of faith and power to sitting and begging God to kill him. That's how far and how quickly he fell.

There's a principle to learn from that account. You will have great victories in God, and you should enjoy them and appreciate them. However, never forget that most great victories are followed by great trials. The fact that you win a battle doesn't mean that Satan will concede the war. He will counterattack, and you have to be ready for that. If you expect to live forever on the mountaintop of your past successes, you'll be caught completely off guard when trouble pulls the rug from under your feet and you begin slipping down the slope of your mountaintop experience. This is what got Elijah into trouble, and that's what happens when you fixate on the wonderful experiences of the past.

It's normal and natural to want to stay on the mountaintop forever, but it's not realistic. Enjoy the time on the top, but never let it lull you to sleep or give you a false sense of security. Never give in to the temptation to think you've "arrived" and can quit warring. In this life, the war will never be over. You will have a breather between battles from time to time, but your enemy, the devil, will *never* stop coming against you. Press on, and don't look back.

Fearfulness and Timidity

A third reason some people don't want to fight is found in Judges 7. In this passage of Scripture, Gideon and his army were poised to fight the Midianites. They were thirty-two thousand strong, ready to go to war against their enemy. God, however, had a different plan in mind to show forth

His glory, so He instructed Gideon, "Whoever is fearful and afraid, let him turn and depart at once from Mount Gilead" (v. 3). With that way out offered, Gideon lost twenty-two thousand men.

Fear and timidity will stop you from pressing forward in battle. Have you ever been standing in faith for a physical healing of some type and someone comes along just to inform you that they know someone who died of that exact thing? You can't afford to embrace that fear, or you'll throw in the towel and the devil will fulfill his evil plan against you.

I've seen this happen in counseling sessions. I once counseled a man who felt called into the ministry, but whose home life was rather unstable. In the course of the session, I told the man the story of a world-famous Bible teacher and what had happened to him. Shortly after this man got saved, his wife abandoned him and their daughter because of his decision to follow the Lord. Because of his wife's decision, this man of God was left alone to follow God and raise his little girl, both of which he did faithfully.

My intention in telling the story was to encourage the man to follow the Lord regardless of the problems he faced, and to show him the difficult choices others had made and how God had sustained them. To my dismay, however, the man couldn't get past the fact that the man's wife had left him. "You mean, his wife left him over the ministry?" he fearfully asked.

"No," I answered, "she left him because he got saved." But in that moment, the devil began whispering to him, "If you go into the ministry, your wife is going to leave you. You'll end up all alone." He latched on to the possibility of what the devil might do instead of the promise of what God would do.

Unfortunately, that's how people are. They will grasp any bad report and take it in until it has them so bound up in fear they can't move. They hear that someone at work has lost his job and immediately assume they're next to get a pink slip. Because of fear, they latch on to a remote possibility. They don't know why that person lost his job, but somehow they just figure they're next.

That's no way to live, brothers and sisters. You've got to remember that God's going to fight for you. Even if you do lose your job, God has a better one for you. He'll just transplant you to another, more fertile part of His garden. You do not operate in the same system as the world, so you don't have to fear what they fear.

Most of the church world is timid and fearful when it comes to spiritual warfare. They take in every bizarre story they've ever heard about the devil until they are paralyzed with fear. They don't dare confront him, because they're afraid of what he might do. If I were to randomly approach two or three Christians and say, "Hey, want to go cast out devils with me?" they'd be likely to say, "Sorry, but I've got to go home." If your pastor asked you to go into the back room of your church and pray for a demon-possessed person, you might suddenly need to go home—or anywhere else!—just not into that room. That's because most of us live in fear of the devil and avoid actively engaging him.

Dependence on Others' Faith

The fourth thing that will cause you not to fight is an overdependence on the faith of others. This will really put you on the back burner in spiritual warfare. In the Old Testament, the story of Barak demonstrates what happens when a person depends on the faith of others. At that time, the prophetess Deborah judged Israel, and one day God gave her a message for Barak. She called him to her and said that God wanted him to take ten thousand men to fight Sisera. God, she assured him, would deliver Israel's enemy into his hands. Now watch what Barak said: "If you will go with me, then I will go; but if you will not go with me, I will not go!"

(Judg. 4:8). He was totally dependent upon Deborah and her ability to touch God in prayer and warfare.

That is exactly what happens to so many Christians. They go through their entire spiritual lives depending on somebody else's faith. If they get sick, they immediately call Sister So-and-So. When their finances dry up, they're on the phone with Brother So-and-So. They have somebody they run to for every problem that comes their way.

It is true that you need others in the body of Christ, and Christians are called to support one another in time of need; however, if you are not careful, you'll grow lazy spiritually and become accustomed to relying on everyone else's faith instead of learning how to flex your own spiritual muscles. I discourage people from doing that. You don't know if that person you depend upon will always be around when you need him. No one but you is responsible for praying through and getting answers to the difficult situations you face. Yes, call upon Christian family and friends, but you take the responsibility for pressing in. Let the faith of others supplement your faith, not replace it.

Barak, obviously, had not yet learned that lesson, so there he was—dependent on Deborah's faith. Deborah did agree to go with him, but look what she said in verse 9: "There will be no glory for you in the journey you are taking, for the Lord will sell Sisera into the hand of a woman." Her words did indeed come to pass when a woman named Jael drove a peg through Sisera's temple (v. 21). Because Barak was living off the faith of others, he was led out by one woman and stood on the sidelines while another killed his enemy.

Compromise with the World

This is the fifth area that can drag people away from the war: compromise with the world. In Judges 2:2–3, the Israelites were severely reproved for failing to destroy all the people of Canaan. Although God had instructed them to annihilate their enemy, they did not heed His voice, and as a result, they had to face the consequences of their disobedience.

The people of Israel, like many of us, got tired of war, so they compromised. They thought it wouldn't hurt to enter into alliances with the Canaanites rather than destroy them. Sometimes this action was initiated by the vanquished foe, who would make an offer of peace in exchange for agreeing to serve the Israelites. Israel, many times, accepted the offer, ignoring the fact that they were failing to carry out God's specific instructions. They thought they could just live in peace and get along with their enemies. They were sadly mistaken, however, because it never works to compromise with the devil and try to make peace with the enemy.

In Judges 2:3, the Angel of the Lord said, "I will not drive them [the enemy] out before you; but they shall be thorns in your side, and their gods shall be a snare to you." When the people of Israel heard this judgment from the Angel of the Lord, they "lifted up their voices and wept. Then they called the name of that place Bochim; and they sacrificed there to the Lord" (vv. 4–5). The name *Bochim* means "weeping," and God's warriors became weepers because they refused to go in and destroy their enemies.

That which you tolerate will end up terrorizing you. You cannot compromise with the devil. Anything less than total annihilation will leave you susceptible to his continuing attacks. It's easy to let this happen in your life. You develop a problem in an area, and you find yourself letting it slide. You never really confront the issue and resolve it; you just hope that somehow it will get better. But it never does; it continues indefinitely, and before you know it, you're weeping. That which you tolerated has now become a terror to you.

Verses 21–22 show how it ended up for Israel. God said, "I will no longer drive out the nations that Joshua left unconquered when he died. I did this to test Israel—to see whether or not they would obey the Lord as their ancestors did" (NLT). God tested Israel and they came up short. Those who came after Joshua failed to continue the battle and win the war that he had begun.

Brothers and sisters, you cannot afford to tolerate anything of the devil. If you have been doing that, start over today. Stop the weeping and become a warrior. Put down the Kleenex and take up your sword. Begin today to press forward in whatever battle you're facing.

It's like trying to open a jammed door. You know the door is unlocked, but something is impeding your progress, so you put your shoulder to it and push and push until the applied pressure forces the door to fly open. That's what spiritual warfare does.

Fighting the enemy is also like moving a stalled vehicle. In the initial moments of trying to move the car, you have no kinetic energy, but as you continue pushing, the car begins to budge just a little. Then it starts moving a little more until it is rolling. At that point, it takes less and less effort from you to keep the car moving.

This is what you and I have got to do. I don't care how long you've been stalled on the highway of life or how long the door to victory has been shut. It's time to rise up in the Spirit and put on your boxing gloves against your foe. Refuse to make a treaty of compromise with him. Serve notice on him that you are going to war against him, you're going to use your authority and weapons, and you're not going to stop until he ceases all his wicked maneuvers.

Worship the Lord, for He is truly your strength and power. You belong to Him, bought by the precious blood of Jesus Christ. Exalt Him with singing, dancing, and with all your body, mind, and spirit. Then after you've worshiped, jump into the fray of battle, sure of victory because of His mighty power residing in you. Call on His name and watch Him save you from every enemy!

Chapter 3

The Coverings of Worship and Submission

You are in a real war against a real enemy. Nevertheless, you have authority over this enemy if you will rise up and use the weapons at your disposal. All that's been covered in the first two chapters. Once you've accepted the basic premise of spiritual warfare, however, you've got to know the specifics that will help you win the war. That's what I am going to address in this chapter.

In any battle, it is important for a soldier to know exactly how to keep himself covered until the moment of attack. He doesn't want the enemy to know his whereabouts ahead of time; he wants to catch the enemy off guard. If he is to be effective in battle, it is imperative that he keep his position concealed until the strategic moment of attack arrives.

This is an important principle to understand in spiritual warfare. You've got to keep spiritually covered; you can't go running around totally exposed on the battlefield, with no armor, no weapons, no covering, and no commander. That would be just as foolhardy and dangerous as it would be for a military soldier to do. God has a spiritual covering for you to wear, and when you do things His way, you protect your-self from many of the enemy's strategies.

The Security of Covering

When we speak about keeping our covering in the Lord, we're basically speaking about a defensive mechanism. We're talking about the way we protect ourselves against the enemy's attack. In Psalm 18:2 KJV, David asserted the Lord's protective presence in his life: "The Lord is my rock, and my fortress, and my deliverer." These are all defensive things. "Rock" refers to an inaccessibly high place where David could be safe. "Fortress" refers to a physical place of defense where David could be secure from the enemy.

The second part of verse 2 continues with additional defensive descriptions of God: ". . . My God, my strength . . . my buckler [shield] . . . the horn of my salvation . . . my high tower." David recognized God as the source of his strength, as a shield of protection, and as the one secure place where he was safe and protected from any enemy. Our attempts to defend ourselves are always limited and never foolproof, but when we look to God for security, we discover that He can completely protect and cover us from any enemy. He is the rock that can never be broken, the fortress that can never be breached, the high tower that can never be taken. David knew that His strength lay in God alone, and time after time in his life, he found himself hiding in that divine protection.

David spent quite a few years of his life running and hiding from Saul. Time after time, Saul's victory over him seemed imminent, but each time David somehow escaped from Saul's grasp. He knew too well what it was like to have a mortal enemy in pursuit and no one to depend upon but God. From those years of running and the resultant develop-ment of his faith in God, David birthed many of the psalms.

When David wrote Psalm 57, he was hiding from Saul in a cave. There in the dark confines of that desolate place, he wrote:

> Be merciful to me, O God, be merciful to me!
> For my soul trusts in You;
> And in the shadow of Your wings I will make my refuge,
> Until these calamities have passed by (v. 1).

Comparing himself to a baby chick that finds shelter under its mother's wings, David affirmed his trust and belief in God. David couldn't trust Saul one bit, but he could trust God totally. He knew that his present calamities wouldn't last forever; they would pass.

That's so important for you to remember. Problems do come, and sometimes they are overwhelming. But no problem lasts forever; it will surely pass, just as surely as the sun rises and sets each day. When you feel like you want to give up, remind yourself "This too shall pass," and when you've done everything you know to do, remember Ephesians 6:13: ". . . having done all, to stand."

Psalm 91 is one of the most famous of David's psalms, and it is a wonderful psalm to read when you feel weak and vulnerable. Verse 1 says:

> He who dwells in the secret place of the Most High
> Shall abide under the shadow of the Almighty.

The word *Almighty* in this verse is translated "El Shaddai" in Hebrew. The Hebrew root, *shad,* means "breast." When David called God "El Shaddai," he was calling Him the "breasted one," the God who wants to bring us close to His bosom and hide us there. There is no safer place to be.

Have you ever seen a mother kangaroo with her baby in her pouch? The young joey is completely hidden from view unless he peeks his bright, inquisitive eyes over the top of the pouch. He is absolutely secure while he is in his mother's pouch, and no one even knows he is there unless he reveals his presence. You are that secure when you live in the shadow of almighty God.

I love the way 1 Samuel 25:29 expresses this same thought. Abigail, wife of Nabal, approached David to make amends for her husband's rude, abrasive behavior. She recognized God's hand of protection upon David and said to him, "Even when you are chased by those who seek your life, you are safe in the care of the Lord your God, secure in his treasure pouch!" (NLT). What a beautiful thought! God holds you in his treasure pouch; you are that valuable to Him.

Some of you reading this book are in the midst of a real battle right now. You don't know how you're going to make it. But I've got good news for you! You *are* going to make it. You're coming through because you hide in the shadow of the Almighty. You are hidden in God's treasure pouch, so how can the devil possibly harm you?

Psalm 91:4 proclaims:

He shall cover you with His feathers,
And under His wings you shall take refuge.

I love that phrase, *He shall cover you*. The Hebrew word used here for *cover* is the same word used of the cherubim that covered the mercy seat of the ark of the covenant. That's how precious you are to God.

When one soldier tells another, "I've got you covered," he means that he will stand guard and watch for the enemy. He will stand poised with his finger on the trigger and will not hesitate to pull it if his comrade is threatened. As dedicated as a soldier may be, he cannot guarantee absolute safety to the one he is trying to cover. But when God covers you, the protection is complete. *Nothing* can reach you without going through Him first.

Living secure in God's love and protection frees you from fear. Fear is a very real problem for many people. They fear they'll get cancer, they fear their children will get killed in a car wreck, they fear they'll lose their jobs, and on the list goes. When you know God has you covered, however, you are not afraid of "the terror by night," "the arrow that flies by day," "the pestilence that walks in darkness," or "the destruction that lays waste at noonday" (vv. 5, 6). Although you recognize all the evil that exists in the world and all the bad things that can happen, your heart is at rest because you have made God your dwelling place.

Although speaking of Jesus, verse 11 of Psalm 91 also applies to us as believers and is a powerful weapon of spiritual warfare:

> For He shall give His angels charge over you,
> To keep you in all your ways.

That, my friend, is better protection than even the best insurance policy. God's got His angels watching over you. They are emissaries sent from God to do His bidding, and one of their jobs is to watch over you!

All this, of course, does not mean that nothing bad can ever touch you. It does mean, however, that you have Someone to walk you through whatever problem comes your way, and it does mean that you have a Father who is looking out for you and who will protect you. God sets the parameters of the trials you face—not Satan—so you can be calm and confident regardless of the external circumstances in your life.

Psalm 140:7 says:

> O God the Lord, the strength of my salvation,
> You have covered my head in the day of battle.

David understood God's covering power better than anyone else. From experience, he had learned how to hide in an impregnable position in God that no enemy could penetrate. Time after time, he had watched God prove Himself strong on his behalf. That's why he could confidently profess his trust in God and endure all that Saul threw at him.

If you're going to make it through life, you have to know the security of God's covering. You have to know that when you are in God, the devil might bark and growl, but he cannot defeat you as long as you stay under God's covering. That covering is composed of four main parts, and the first of these is worship.

The Covering of Worship

As mentioned in the previous chapter, worship is our primary weapon in spiritual warfare. When we loose it, we loose God's delivering power on our behalf. In addition to being an offensive weapon at our disposal, however, worship is also part of our defensive covering.

In 1 Samuel 15, Saul fell from favor with God because of disobedience. Samuel the prophet mourned for Saul until God told him it was time to move on and select the one who would eventually become Israel's king. The first half of 1 Samuel 16 chronicles David's selection by Samuel as king of Israel, and the second half of the chapter sets the stage for the ensuing conflict between Saul and David. At this point in Scripture, we see the role of worship as a spiritual covering.

Because of Saul's rebellion, God allowed a tormenting spirit to come upon him, a spirit that "filled him with depression and fear" (v. 14 NLT). When this spirit descended upon Saul, he became quite distressed and agitated. His servants suggested a remedy: to find someone who could play the harp and soothe Saul's troubled mind when the spirit came upon him. Saul agreed to the solution, and "it just so happened" that one of the servants recommended David, the shepherd boy. The servant described him as "skillful in playing, a mighty man of valor, a man of war, prudent in speech, and a handsome person; and the Lord is with him" (v. 18).

While David was alone with his sheep, God had been grooming him for his future. Those lonely days spent strumming his harp and singing songs from his heart suddenly catapulted him into the king's palace. God was at work.

Handpicked by the Lord for this task, David was instrumental in restoring peace to the tormented king's mind. Verse 23 says, "And so it was, whenever the spirit from God was upon Saul, that David would take a harp and play it with his hand. Then Saul would become refreshed and well, and the distressing spirit would depart from him."

This remarkable account in the Bible is the only instance in the Old Testament of demonic deliverance. Isn't it interesting that it happened through the medium of worship and praise? As David strummed his harp and sang of God's wonders, the high praises of God filled the room. Saul, the tormented king, was refreshed and his sanity temporarily restored.

By the time we come to chapter 18 in 1 Samuel, David had moved into the palace, formed a friendship with Saul's son Jonathan, and become commander of the army. Everything he did succeeded, and his fame increased among the people. When the women began singing and boasting of David's superior military prowess, however, Saul was provoked to jealousy, and the very next day the evil spirit returned (vv. 7–10). (Notice the connection between Saul's jealousy and the spirit's return.)

At first everything seemed to proceed as usual. The tormenting spirit gripped Saul, and David was called to play his harp. "David played music with his hand, as at other times; but there was a spear in Saul's hand. And Saul cast the spear, for he said, 'I will pin David to the wall!' But David escaped his presence twice" (vv. 10, 11). Twice! That means that after Saul's first attempt to kill him, David just picked up his harp and went right back to strumming. He knew his head was covered; he knew who his rock was; he knew he was secure in his high tower.

Few of us would have faulted David for leaving Saul permanently after being attacked in that way. In our eyes, he would have been totally justified, but this was not God's plan. David thus remained submitted to Saul and stayed with him a while longer.

After this episode, David and Saul managed to patch up their differences (1 Sam. 19:4–7). The tormenting spirit, however, would have none of this and eventually returned and enticed Saul to try again to kill David (vv. 9–10). This time David was forced to flee, and his years of running from Saul began that night.

David escaped to the prophet Samuel, and the two of them went to Naioth. Saul, still in a rage, sent soldiers there to capture David. When the soldiers arrived, however, they saw Samuel and the other prophets prophesying, and before they knew it, they were prophesying too (vv. 18–20)!

Twice more Saul sent troops to capture David, but both times they only ended up prophesying under the anointing of the Spirit of the Lord. Saul finally had had enough of that, so he decided to capture David himself. When he arrived at Naioth, however, the Spirit of God came upon him so strongly that he prostrated himself before Samuel and prophesied for twenty-four hours (vv. 21–24).

How powerful is the secret place of the Most High! It can overcome any intention of man, any demonic scheme, and even the strongest army. Nothing could hurt David because he was hidden in the secret place of God, and worship was the key to entering that place of covering.

The Power of Worship

I remember once experiencing the covering of worship in a most powerful way. In 1975, I took my first trip behind the Iron Curtain. This occurred before the fall of communism in Eastern Europe, so traveling there as a young man was quite an experience for me and the other young men with me. As we approached the border crossing into Romania, we were quite nervous because we were carrying in Bibles for the people we were going to visit.

When we came to the crossing, the first thing we were required to do was to drive the car over a trough filled with water and sit there for ten minutes. This was to make sure that we were not trying to smuggle someone in. We made it through that point but noticed the guards carefully examining all the vehicles. We watched them take out seats and inspect practically every inch of the vehicles, so thorough were they in their search for illegal people or items.

I remember being very scared and thinking silly, nervous thoughts. "Lord, if I'm not saved, I want to get saved right now! If I have any sin in my life, I confess it doubly right now," I fervently prayed. In the midst of this emotional turmoil, the Lord assured me that He was going to cover our heads in the day of battle.

My traveling companions and I began to praise and worship God as we waited in line for our turn to cross. We made a conscious decision to worship and turned our focus to the Lord, singing praises to Him and reminding ourselves of His might and power. I'm not saying it was easy, but it was what we chose to do.

Too quickly our turn arrived. A guard took our passports and then ordered everyone out of the car. He walked around to the trunk to examine its contents, and we got even more nervous because that is where the Bibles were, hidden under a pink blanket. One blanket does not offer much protection, so we knew we were in trouble unless God helped us.

We held our breath and did our best to continue worshiping in our hearts as the guard began his search. He proceeded to lift the blanket and look inside the trunk for a minute before putting the blanket down. Then he closed the trunk and instructed us to get back into the car. Returning our passports, he waved us through the checkpoint, wishing us a good visit to Romania!

When my friends and I got about half a mile down the road, we stopped the car and began wildly praising the God who had covered our heads in battle. We had no idea what the guard had seen or not seen; all we knew was that God had fought for us while we kept our hearts in praise and worship. That is the covering that worship brings.

Worship really was one of David's most powerful tools in his struggle with Saul. Saul was a dogged foe, determined to kill David if it was the last thing he did. Because of the demented king, David's life drastically changed from serving in the king's palace and army to living as a fugitive. Prestige and position were stripped from him, and he was forced to run for his life. First Samuel 23:14 says, "David stayed in strongholds in the wilderness, and remained in the mountains in the Wilderness of Ziph. Saul sought him every day, but God did not deliver him into his hand."

That was David's life—always looking over his shoulder, always on guard, always running. There was no rest from Saul's pursuit. Every time David escaped to one place, Saul found him. When David ran from that place, Saul found him again. On and on it went, but Saul could never catch David because God was covering him.

That's important for you to remember when you are facing a trial. No problem, temptation, or demon can gain the upper hand if you will remain under God's covering. It doesn't matter how many times the devil attacks or what he does. God is in control, and nothing can stop His eternal purposes from coming to pass.

Finally the day came that seemed like a golden opportunity for David to get rid of Saul once and for all. As David and his men hid in a cave, who should come in but Saul himself, totally unaware of their presence! Their archenemy was literally in their trap. All they had to do was spring the latch and Saul would be theirs.

In verse 4 of 1 Samuel 24, "The men of David said to him, 'This is the day of which the Lord said to you, "Behold, I will deliver your enemy into your hand, that you may do to him as it seems good to you." ' " But all David did was creep forward and cut off a small piece of Saul's garment, and even that action pricked his conscience. "And he said to his men, 'The Lord forbid that I should do this thing to my master, the Lord's anointed, to stretch out my hand against him, seeing he is the anointed of the Lord' " (v. 5).

This was a critical juncture in David's life. David refused to touch the Lord's anointed, even though Saul was so obviously in the wrong and had been rejected by God. Still, God had not yet chosen to remove Saul from power, and David was loath to do so. He knew where his lines of authority were drawn, and he refused to step across those boundaries. He respected Saul's position as king and left the dealing of Saul to the Lord. David stayed under the covering of submission.

The Covering of Submission

Submission is something the devil knows nothing about. His entire career began in rebellion, so he understands nothing about submission. He tries his best to lure you out of the covered place of submission to God and to entice you to take matters into your own hands. That will always get you into trouble. Stay covered, and wait for God's vindication.

Don't give in to the temptation to take matters into your own hands, no matter how justified you might feel in doing so.

In 1 Samuel 26, the story of David and Saul continues. This was the last time David saw Saul. The circumstances were so familiar: David hiding, Saul chasing, David getting the opportunity to kill Saul, David again refusing to touch the Lord's anointed. The submission in David's heart to both God and Saul reigned supreme. Twice he could have killed Saul, but instead he remained submitted. God had not given him permission to destroy his enemy; God would deal with Saul in His own way and in His own time, and David knew this (vv. 9–11). So David stayed under God's covering, worshiping and serving Him, and left Saul to God.

From this point on in Scripture, we never see David and Saul interacting again. Saul eventually met a tragic death, never recovering from the evil possession that had engulfed him. When he finally died, David wept and lamented for him. He even composed a funeral song and ordered all Israel to sing it (2 Sam. 1:17–18). To the very end, David was loyal to Saul and submitted to his authority. He never took vengeance into his own hands, and even when God's judgment fell on his enemy, it brought him no joy. He wept for what had become of Saul: "How the mighty have fallen!" (v. 27).

The two guiding principles in David's life were worship and submission. As long as he worshiped God, the Lord delivered him. As long as he remained submitted to God, His covering was secure. As long as you remain submitted to God, your covering is secure too. But if you walk in intentional disobedience and rebellion, you walk out from under your covering.

That's what Lucifer (Satan) did. Ezekiel 28:13 gives a description of Lucifer and his fall from heaven:

You were in Eden, the garden of God;
Every precious stone was your covering:
The sardius, topaz, and diamond,
Beryl, onyx, and jasper,
Sapphire, turquoise, and emerald with gold.
The workmanship of your timbrels and pipes
Was prepared for you on the day you were created.

The Word of God says the devil was covered with precious stones. His covering was absolutely gorgeous, and because verse 13 refers to timbrels and pipes (musical instruments), many scholars also believe that Lucifer led worship in heaven.

Apparently that was not enough for Lucifer. Puffed up with pride, he instigated a futile rebellion against God (v. 17). As a result, he was stripped of his beautiful covering and all it signified. He was cast to the earth, fallen, stripped, and devoid of the ability to worship. From that point on, the history of the human race has centered around whom we will worship.

In the Garden of Eden, Adam and Eve were protected as long as they remained submitted to God and under His covering. They worshiped Him and walked in daily communion with Him. Even though they were naked, they had no sense of being uncovered, because they dwelt in the shadow of the Almighty, safe under His wings. Theirs was a life of fulfillment, praise, and worship—totally submitted to God and thus totally covered and totally safe.

When they sinned, however, everything changed. They moved out from under their covering and immediately recognized their nakedness. Uncovered, vulnerable, and ashamed, they feebly tried to cover themselves with fig leaves. This, of course, could not suffice, so God graciously provided a way for them to be adequately covered. "And the Lord God made clothing from animal skins for Adam and his wife" (Gen.

3:21 NIV). The Lord took a blood sacrifice from animals and covered Adam and Eve in the skins from that sacrifice, a type of atonement that pointed ahead to Jesus' sacrificial death on the cross.

Submission to proper authority is very important in spiritual warfare. Rebellious people who refuse to live under God's authority are constantly fighting the devil. But if you know how to keep your head covered through submission, you're protected in the battle.

It's like the story a pastor friend once told me. Growing up as a country boy, he lived in a house without screens on the windows. Flies were everywhere, needless to say. My friend said that his father carried a flyswatter around and constantly battled the flies. He did the best he could, but as soon as he got rid of all the flies he could find, more came in. They were just a fact of life in the country. Then one day the family purchased screens for the windows. Suddenly his daddy didn't have to spend all his time swatting flies, because the screens had eliminated most of them. A few got in every now and then, but the constant battling with them was over.

A lot of believers spend their time swatting flies. The devil attacks here, and they bring the flyswatter down. They kill that fly, but another one starts buzzing around. They kill that one, and then here comes another one. They have no screens, nothing to cover their windows to keep out the flies. As a result, they have no rest or peace because they have no covering. They're leaving the spiritual windows open and exposed by not using the coverings of worship and submission.

Jesus' Perfect Submission

First Corinthians 11:3 states, "The head of every man is Christ, the head of woman is man, and the head of Christ is God." Jesus, of course, is equal with God, because He is God made flesh, yet He willingly submitted Himself to the Father.

His entire earthly ministry was submitted to the Father's will. He did nothing of His own accord and acknowledged the Father as the head.

For forty days and nights in the wilderness, Jesus fasted. Anyone would be famished at the end of forty days without food, and Jesus, being fully man, had a physical body with real limitations. By the time forty days had elapsed, He was hungry (Luke 4:2).

At that point of physical vulnerability, the devil appeared and whispered, "Why don't you turn some stones into bread?" Isn't that just like him, to attack at Jesus' weakest moment? He'll try the same tactic with you. He knows when you have endured about as much as you think you can stand, and just at that moment, he'll move in for the kill.

Jesus, however, did nothing except what the Father instructed. Remaining in perfect submission and ignoring the physical demands of His body, He countered the devil's temptation with the Word of God: "It is written, 'Man shall not live by bread alone, but by every word of God' " (Luke 4:4). The devil came with two more temptations, but both times Jesus pulled out the sword of the Word of God and held firm.

Following His testing in the desert, Jesus began His public ministry. One day in the synagogue in Nazareth, Jesus stood and read from Isaiah, "The Spirit of the Lord is upon Me. . . ." (v. 18). After listening to Jesus apply this passage to Himself and reprimand them for their lack of faith, the people became infuriated "and rose up and thrust Him out of the city; and they led Him to the brow of the hill on which their city was built, that they might throw Him down over the cliff" (v. 29).

But look what happened next: "Then passing through the midst of them, He went His way" (v. 30). Something supernatural happened. Here was Jesus, the seeming victim of mob mentality, and just when the people were ready to shove Him off the cliff, He somehow walked away. That "somehow" that kept Jesus from harm, I believe, was His covering in God. He knew how to abide in the secret place, and He never deviated from following the Father's will.

The devil cannot destroy you—even if he brings you to the edge of the cliff—if God's not through with you yet. God ordained your beginning, and God ordains your end. In Him you are perfectly protected, as long as you continue worshiping, abiding in the shadow of His wings, and resting in submission. There is no safer place than the Father's will for your life.

The cross declares Jesus' ultimate act of submission to the Father. Hebrews 2:9 says, "We see Jesus, who was made a little lower than the angels, for the suffering of death crowned with glory and honor." Right up to the point of crucifixion, Jesus was saying, "Not My will, but Yours." His unwavering submission was His victory, and it ultimately brought Him eternal glory and honor. None of it, though, would have happened without His submission.

Because of Jesus' obedience to the Father's will, He destroyed "him who had the power of death, that is, the devil, and release[d] those who through fear of death were all their lifetime subject to bondage" (vv. 14, 15). His death utterly destroyed Satan's power once and for all, and even the ultimate enemy, death, was defeated. All this is yours, if you will stay in that place of safety found in submission to God. Be forewarned, however, that if you persist in rebellion, purposefully disobeying Him and consciously removing yourself from His covering, then you are vulnerable to whatever the devil wants to throw your way. Your covering is dependent upon the submission of your body, mind, and spirit to the will of God.

Submit Your Body

Romans 6:12 admonishes us not to let sin reign in our bodies, but instead to surrender ourselves to God and use our bodies as instruments, or weapons, of righteousness. That means that if you will yield your body to God every day, sin will be crucified in you and you won't have to be a slave to it anymore. That, of course, is a lifetime process, but gradually you should become more and more like Jesus. Each day give God your hands, your eyes, your tongue, your feet, and every part of your body. Yield yourself to service, purity, and holiness.

When somebody puts a gun to your back and says, "Stick 'em up!" you lift your hands in submission. When you lift your hands in worship, you're using your body to represent your total submission to God. You're coming under His covering and acknowledging His headship. It's a symbol of a surrender that is taking place in the heart.

Jesus said if your right hand causes you to sin, cut it off. This is not a literal admonition, but it stresses the point that it would be better to end up in heaven with one hand than to go to hell with two. Take whatever measures necessary to keep your body surrendered to God and His will. Don't let your feet take you into places you have no business going. Keep your hands from touching anything unclean and your eyes from looking at pornography. Put a muzzle on your mouth if you have to, to keep yourself from saying mean-spirited, hurtful things that you will regret. Keep your body submitted to God, His will, and His call to holiness.

Submit Your Mind

You also have to yield your mind to God. Second Corinthians 10:4–5 KJV states, "The weapons of our warfare are not carnal, but mighty through God to the pulling down of strong holds; casting down imaginations, and every high thing that exalteth itself against the knowledge of God, and bringing into captivity every thought to the obedience of Christ."

That is perhaps one of the most powerful verses in the New Testament. You have a supernatural weapon to use whenever the devil fires a dart at your mind. You don't have to remain a victim of endless mind-games that distract and torment. Through the Word of God, you can cast down imaginations, things that pop into your mind that have absolutely no basis.

When you find yourself thinking, "My spouse doesn't really love me," recognize it for what it is—an imagination—and immediately discard it. Don't entertain it, but take it captive, just like enemy soldiers are captured in a war. Seize every thought that is contrary to the knowledge of God and make it line up in proper submission to Jesus Christ. That's how to keep your mind submitted.

Submit Your Spirit

In addition to keeping your body and mind submitted, you must keep your spirit submitted to Christ. First Peter 5:5 says to submit to others in the body of Christ, remembering that God resists those who are proud but gives grace to those who are humble.

This refers to spiritual authority in your life. When you commit yourself to a local church and plant yourself there, you are under its spiritual covering. This is a very serious matter, so don't put yourself under spiritual authority that you do not respect or that violates God's Word. Find a clean, pure church that preaches the Gospel clearly and unashamedly, and submit yourself under that.

Spiritual submission applies not only to church members but also to pastors. Pastors need to be submitted to a group of men who will lend oversight and guard them from doctrinal or moral error. I am so persuaded of the importance of doing this that for years I have submitted the ministry of Bethany to a group of presbyters over me. Everyone needs to be in submission to someone. I am no exception, and neither are you.

Submission requires humility, but verses 6–7 of 1 Peter 5 tell us the results of it: "Humble yourselves under the mighty hand of God that He may exalt you in due time, casting all your care upon Him, for He cares for you." Verse 8 continues, "Be sober, be vigilant; because your adversary the devil walks about like a roaring lion, seeking whom he may devour." There is a clear connection between walking in humility and submission, and the devil's ability to devour you.

Some of you are in the midst of a real battle. Your submission to God is key to your victory. Don't decide you've got to take matters into your own hands. Don't decide you can't praise and worship God anymore. Remain under God's covering, and stay under the protection of your local church. Submit to God first and then resist the devil; once you get the sequence flowing, the devil has no choice but to flee (v. 7).

I once dreamed that I was in a church in Indonesia and heard a man preaching under a high anointing. This preacher walked over to a man who was demon-possessed in order to lay hands on him. As he approached the man, however, the man began backing up. Every time the preacher moved forward, the man moved backward, and this sequence went on for a little while. Then the preacher turned to the congregation and said, "See? See the authority we have?" Then the preacher caught up with the man and pulled a shadow-like figure out of him, held it by the nape of the neck and the seat of the pants, walked the figure to the back door, and just threw it out. He walked back to the man, grabbed another figure, and did the same thing. Then he turned to the congregation and said, "You see how easy this is?" That's authority in action!

Some of you have been swatting flies for too long—it's time to put up the screens. Some of you have left your head exposed—it's time to come back under God's covering in the secret place. Some of you have grown disillusioned and left the protection of the local church—it's time to submit yourself again to others in the Lord. In whatever area you may have given the devil entrance, you can begin to resist him today. When you do, you can be sure he will flee. That's the authority you have when you remain under God's holy coverings of worship and submission.

Chapter 4

The Coverings of Divine Order and Love

The next two ways we keep covered in spiritual warfare are through divine order and love. Let's take divine order first. This particular aspect of God's covering is not always popular or fashionable to teach, but it is a very real and valuable part of God's plan to keep us covered in the day of battle.

All of God's creation is under divine order. The planets, the stars, and everything on earth operate according to God's natural laws that He has set into place. These things are necessary for the orderly flow of life. They are not bad things, but exist to bring peace and order to the universe. Without them, chaos would rule.

In the same way, God has established a divine order in relationships, and 1 Corinthians 11:3 distinctly explains it. This verse says, "I want you to know that the head of every man is Christ, the head of woman is man, and the head of Christ is God." God the Father is the head of Christ, who is the head of man, who is the head of woman. This order in no way indicates superiority of the Father over the Son or the man over the woman. God is not more important than

Christ (they are one), and man is not more important than the woman (they are joint-heirs). The designated positions exist simply to allow divine order to flow.

Satan always tries to disrupt divine order. In the desert, he tried to persuade Jesus to rebel against God's headship, but he failed miserably. He tries to entice each of us to live according to our own plans instead of God's, telling us we don't need to submit to God. If he can't succeed there, he will try to tempt us to rebel against the divine order God has placed in the home.

Divine Order for Married Couples

The entire subject of divine order in the home has been the source of much misunderstanding, not only among unbelievers but also among Christians. The Bible never teaches that woman is to be under the foot of man so that he can step on her. She is never meant to be a doormat, subject to the every whim of a selfish man. Eve, the first woman, was taken from Adam's rib, from under his heart, because she was meant to walk side by side with him under the protection of his arm.

For the purpose of order, the man is the "coverer" for his family. That means he is to protect his wife and children both spiritually and physically. An emotionally healthy man possesses a basic sense of security that draws out his natural protectiveness toward his family, but the enemy seeks to undermine this so the man will not use it or the woman will not value it.

I believe that most of the problems that arise in the home stem from the fact that most men have not covered their wives or loved them as Christ loved the church (Eph. 5:25). A man who tries to assume headship over his wife without loving her is actually perverting the Scriptures. God did not make dictators to rule families—he made husbands. He made men to cover, protect, and provide for their wives. That means, husbands, if you hear something in the night, you're the one who gets up and looks into it. You're not supposed to pull the covers over your head and tell your wife, "Go get 'em, honey!" You be the protector, even if you're scared.

A man must also protect his wife spiritually. When a man is right with God, a protective covering rests over his family; when he is not walking with God, his family is more vulnerable to the enemy's attacks. Each person, of course, is responsible for his own individual walk with the Lord, but there is something about a husband who takes his rightful place in the home that brings a greater degree of protection to the entire family.

We see this protective aspect of covering beautifully illustrated in the Old Testament story of Ruth. When Ruth approached Boaz, notice her entreaty: "Spread the corner of your *covering* over me, for you are my family redeemer" (Ruth 3:9 NLT, emphasis added). In Jewish culture, when a man stated his intention to take a woman as his wife, he spread his garment over her. That meant she was covered in his protection. No one else could have her because she was under his mantle.

Although Boaz did take his coat and spread it over Ruth, I find it interesting that she initiated the request for covering. I might be stepping out on a limb, but I believe that most women, because of the way God made them, desire to be covered by a husband. This is not to imply in any way that they are less than men or inferior; it is simply a statement of the way God made women for the sake of divine order. They want to be covered, and men who understand this and do this have happy homes.

First Corinthians 11:7 explains, "For a man indeed ought not to cover his head, since he is the image and glory of God; but woman is the glory of man." Here again we see the divine order that God established. Man was made in the image of God, and woman was taken from man. I cannot stress enough that this has nothing to do with superiority. God does not love or accept men more than He does women. That is a ridiculous notion. Any differences between the sexes exist strictly for the purposes of order and the peaceful operation of the home. Anytime a man lords it over his wife in the name of spiritual authority, he has missed the point of divine order and is actually abusing his position.

There is a real trend in our society to downplay the innate differences between men and women. Somehow it has become quite unpopular to voice the belief that there are valid, real differences between the sexes. To do so is to risk being labeled chauvinistic, narrow-minded, and unenlightened.

God's Word, however, never promotes the idea that men and women are exactly the same. The Word of God celebrates the differences and shows us the peace and order that come when all members of a family assume the roles that God made for them. The sooner a woman accepts the fact that God made her to be covered and the sooner a man accepts his responsibility to cover his wife, the sooner their family will flow in harmony and divine order.

There is something amiss in our society when so many men think nothing of reneging on their responsibility to guide and govern their families. They find it so much easier to relinquish that duty to their wives. They would rather let their wives make all the decisions, take care of problems with the children, keep up the house, and do all the myriad of things required in a home. They really don't want to step up to the plate and say to their wives, "Here, honey, let me handle that. You don't have to worry about it; I'll take care of it." No, it's easier to say, "Yes, dear. Whatever you want, dear, is fine with me."

Many women who are leading their homes have been forced into that position. It's the only way the bills get paid, the children fed, and the lawn mowed. It is certainly not the best way and it is not God's way, but sometimes it's the only way a woman can survive. If her husband is content to float merrily along through life, totally oblivious to what is going on in his family, she is forced to step up to the plate.

This passivity on the part of men has unfortunately overflowed into the church. Look around and you'll probably see more women than men in your church volunteering in lay ministry, teaching the children, or leading small groups. Spiritually, as well as physically and emotionally, many men find it easier to abdicate authority rather than assume their God-given roles as protectors and coverers of their families.

If you are a man reading this book, you might object, "But my wife won't accept my headship. She doesn't want to give up control." That may be true to a degree. If your wife has been forced to lead for many years, it will take a period of adjustment for roles in the home to realign in proper balance. However, if you are sincere in your desire to cover your home, your wife will eventually be glad to come under your covering as you prove yourself and your intentions.

Even if your wife refuses to come under your covering, you will still be obeying God's Word and doing what you are supposed to be doing. You can't change anyone; only God can do that. You can't make your wife receive your covering. Forced authority is no authority. If your wife resists your headship, she is resisting God and will have to answer to Him. You continue doing what you know to be right, loving your wife and guiding your family, and leave your wife to God.

Ladies, if your husband is sincerely, genuinely trying to lead your family, you are going to have to learn how to surrender to his headship. It may be especially hard if he has never assumed responsibility before, but just like your husband must obey God's Word, so must you. Your husband may make a mistake or two as he is learning to lead, but if you will remain submitted in your heart and actions, then

God will cover you through your husband's authority. The devil will constantly try to get you to buck your husband's authority, but if you do, you'll find yourself out from under his covering, confused, frightened, and insecure.

Divine Order for Single Women

Women do not have to be married in order to lead fruitful, productive lives in Christ. Single women have opportunities to serve God and wholeheartedly follow Him that married women sometimes do not have. However, I believe that most single Christian women do desire to marry at some point, and though some might disagree, I think this is because of a natural God-given desire within them for covering.

If you are a single woman resistant to the idea of sharing your life with a man, search your heart. Perhaps there is an unhealed wound that affects your ability to relate to men. Perhaps it is a matter of control. Maybe you think a husband would cramp your style. Neither you nor I have the right to dictate to God what we will or will not do, and if God wants to make marriage a part of your future, then you have to be open to that.

I realize how old-fashioned such ideas sound, but they are principles from God's Word. First Peter 3:6 says, "Sarah obeyed Abraham, calling him lord, whose daughters you are if you do good and are not afraid with any terror." A woman submitted to God does not have to be afraid of losing her independence or identity to a man in marriage. When she is under both God's and her husband's coverings, she is protected.

The question remains of who provides covering for a single woman. That is a valid question that deserves an answer. For the woman who is single, the local church is the source of her covering. To the church she should go for the counsel, direction, and help that a husband would normally provide. In particular, she needs to form relationships with older women in the body of Christ who demonstrate solid faith and godly qualities. These women can provide the mentoring relationships that she needs as a single woman.

Titus 2:4–5 NIV instructs the older women in the church to "train the younger women to love their husbands and children, to be self-controlled and pure, to be busy at home, to be kind, and to be subject to their husbands, so that no one will malign the word of God." This is the role of the older women, and this is where the single woman needs to look for help. The maturity and wisdom of women of God who have walked uprightly for many years are invaluable to the young woman trying to figure out what it means to be a godly woman. This is what will protect her from the devil's wiles.

Divine Order for Children

Children, like married and single women, also need a covering, and this they find in their parents. Ephesians 6:1 says, "Children, obey your parents in the Lord, for this is right." Parents are the acknowledged head of the children, and the Scriptures illustrate this principle many times.

In Matthew 15:21–28, for example, a Gentile woman implored Jesus to heal her demon-possessed daughter. Jesus did not even answer her at first, but because of the woman's persistence, He granted the request. Jesus honored this woman's great faith by granting her petition for something her daughter needed. Her faith covered her daughter, who obviously was in no condition to seek healing for herself.

This account from the Bible teaches us that we have a covering over those who are under our authority. We have the ability to exercise our faith, rebuke the devil, and take authority over his work in our children's lives. We are responsible to cover them spiritually; they need the protection that we can afford them as their parents.

Mark 9 reveals another story of a parent's covering over his child. In this account, a man brought his mute, demon-possessed son to Jesus for deliverance (v. 17). Jesus asked the man if he believed that He could heal his son, and in verse 24 the man answered, "Lord, I believe; help my unbelief!" Even with this father's faith being less than perfect, Jesus responded and healed the boy. Again, a parent's faith was the key to a miracle for a child.

Luke 8:41 begins yet another story of a parent's covering. This is the story of Jairus's daughter, who died but was raised from the dead. The little girl was dead, so obviously she couldn't believe for her healing. But Jairus's daughter was under her father's covering, in his sphere of influence, and he had a right to petition Jesus on her behalf. When he exercised that right, his little girl was raised from the dead and one of the greatest miracles of the New Testament occurred.

Parents' authority over their children is just as valid today as it was in Bible days. A Bible teacher I know has often told the story about praying for several years for his daughter, who had warts all over her body. One day while in prayer, he had a vision. Standing before him in his living room was Jesus, who said, "How long are you going to allow those warts on your daughter's body?"

Puzzled, the father responded, "Well, Lord, I thought You would take care of that."

Jesus answered, "No, you're the head of your household. Be the head of your household." Then He disappeared.

This concerned father and godly man began doing what Jesus had instructed him to do. Every day for forty days, he told the devil, "Devil, I am the head of this household, so take your warts out of my house!" On the fortieth day, his daughter came in from school and went into her room. Suddenly her father heard a commotion, and the daughter came running out of her room, screaming, "Daddy, Daddy! I'm getting new skin on my hands!" As he looked at her hands, the warts were disappearing and new skin was forming. God completed the healing, and this young girl was miraculously healed of every wart on her body.

I, too, have had personal experiences with my children in which my authority as their parent released divine healing. I especially remember when my oldest son, Joel, was born. Both of his feet were turned inward, and the doctors decided we needed to put casts on them to correct the alignment. They said he would need several casts, followed by corrective shoes, until he was about two years old. My wife, Melanie, and I did what the doctors recommended, but then we went home and began to pray, spreading our spiritual covering over our tiny, firstborn son.

As I was praying for my son one day, the Lord impressed me with the names of three people that I had never forgiven. I thought that I had forgiven them, but God showed me that I had been holding something against them. Because I still felt pain when I thought of them, I realized that something was not right in my heart. So one by one, I forgave those people from my past. When I finished, I felt a tremendous release and sensed that little Joel had gotten his miracle.

I then went home and told Melanie to remove the casts from Joel's feet. Joel was only three months old at the time, and Melanie brought him into the bathroom and carefully soaked his legs in the tub. The casts soon softened, and as we removed them, we caught our first glimpse of Joel's little feet—perfectly straight! We rejoiced and never even returned to the doctor.

That's the kind of authority parents have over their children. If your children are sick or needy, you can cover them spiritually and command the devil to loose them. But *you* have to rise up and use your authority. *You* have to persevere and refuse to give up. *You* have to believe and ask God to help your unbelief. Regardless of what your children are facing, you can cover them in prayer and intercession.

The Covering of Love

The final covering we are going to talk about is the covering of love. We've studied the protection that worship gives, discussed the safety in submission, and looked at the power of divine order. Now it's time to examine the role of love as a divine covering from the Lord. First Thessalonians 5:8 NIV says, "Let us be self-controlled, putting on faith and love as a breastplate, and the hope of salvation as a helmet." Faith, of course, is important, and this verse tells us it is part of the breastplate that protects our heart. The breastplate, however, includes another component, and that component is love.

Love and Forgiveness

Love and forgiveness go hand in hand, so when you move into unforgiveness, love goes out the window. When unforgiveness takes up residence in your heart, you have actually opened a door that gives the devil every right to enter. That's because you've stopped walking in love and lost part of the protection of your breastplate.

In 2 Corinthians 2, Paul wrote to the church concerning a member who had fallen into sin. Recognizing the danger of withholding forgiveness, Paul wrote this to the Corinthians: "When you forgive this man, I forgive him, too. And when I forgive him (for whatever is to be forgiven), I do so with Christ's authority for your benefit, *so that Satan will not outsmart us*. For we are very familiar with his evil schemes" (vv. 10–11 NLT, emphasis added).

The connection between unforgiveness and giving room to the devil is obvious from these verses. When you forgive, you close a spiritual gap, thus giving Satan no means of entry. When you refuse to forgive, you play directly into the devil's hands and allow him to outsmart you. The same principle applies in a church, family, job, or any other area of life. When you refuse to forgive, you're fair game to the devil. You can rebuke him, quote Scripture, bind and loose, and do everything else you've ever heard about, but the devil has a legal right to remain. Until you forgive, you've lost the protective covering of Christian love.

Ephesians 4:26–27 NLT says, "Don't sin by letting anger gain control over you. Don't let the sun go down while you are still angry, for anger gives a mighty foothold to the Devil." Anger and unforgiveness often go together. Where you find one, the other is usually lurking.

When you become angry with someone, you cannot afford to nurse the offense. Don't give in to the temptation to harbor it for "just a little while." You would be better off calling the one you're upset with and talking the thing out—even if it means humiliating yourself—than holding it close and allowing the devil entry through unforgiveness. That way you keep the breastplate of love intact.

The devil knows nothing about love. All he knows is hate, strife, dissension, and confusion. These are the tools of his trade, and he loves to use them in relationships. He delights to pit one person against another, and he loves to whisper accusations in your ear. "Do you see that person? He's spreading lies about you all over the church," he whispers. In the meantime, he's whispering to the other person about you, "Do you see that person? He's telling lies about you to everybody." Before you realize it, you're both suspicious of each other, and you've erected a wall in your heart between you and your brother or sister in the body of Christ.

Love and Words

It is imperative to give the devil no opportunity to stir up dissension. One primary way that we fail in this area is by not guarding the words we say. Ephesians 4:29 NLT says, "Let everything you say be good and helpful, so that your words will be an encouragement to those who hear them."

When you exchange words that are full of the devil's poison, however, you break the spiritual covering of love.

This happens so frequently in the home. It can begin with something trivial, but when harsh words are spoken, the little problem quickly intensifies into a bigger one. Sometimes I'll decide to "help" Melanie with the dishes, so I'll load the dishwasher after dinner. The only problem is, I don't do it the way she likes, and she'll walk by and innocently say, "Oh, darling, thank you so much for all your help, but let's do it this way." Now Melanie knows a lot more about washing dishes than I do, so her way is better, but if I get all huffy and storm out of the room, saying, "Do it yourself, then, and don't ever expect me to help again!" I've started a war with a few ill-chosen words.

It doesn't matter who "started" the altercation. You choose the words you will or will not say, and you live with the consequences of those words. When I choose to snap at my wife for some innocent comment she made about the dishes, Satan's icy fingers begin creeping into my home. The Holy Spirit retreats, and the devil slinks in. Spiritually I feel naked because I've lost the covering of love. Peace and joy fly out the window, and strife and confusion come barreling through the door.

The funny thing about poorly chosen words is that they seem to grow and escalate. If you storm out of the room when your wife tries to show you a better way to do the dishes, she will probably take it personally and say something like, "I can see that I am not appreciated around here." You reply, "You criticize everything I do; I don't know if you really even loved me when we got married." Before you know it, she's replying, "Well, maybe I didn't; in fact, Mama just called and I think I'll go home for a few days."

All that happens just because she wanted to rearrange the dishes! No dish is worth that. What difference does it really make how the dishwasher is loaded? As long as the dishes get clean, who cares how it happens? Let her hang the dishes from the ceiling and spray them off with a hose, if she wants. *It doesn't matter!*

Resist the urge to say anything and everything that pops into your head. When your wife has a better way of doing things, be glad you have such a smart wife and compliment her on it. Do whatever it takes to keep the covering of love in place in your home.

If you and your spouse will both make the effort to speak good things to each other, you'll change the whole atmosphere of your home. When you speak good words, you build the hedge of protection around your home; when you speak angry words, you tear down the hedge and expose your family to the devil's tactics. Husbands and wives, outdo one another in speaking love, encouragement, and blessing. Build up the wall protecting your family; build it so high the devil can never scale it.

Love and Confession of Sin

Another part of keeping spiritually covered in love is found in James 5:16 NIV: "Confess your sins to each other and pray for each other so that you may be healed." Confession of sins and faults to one another blocks the devil's entrance. I have found that if I offend someone but humble myself to go to him and confess my sin, the problem will generally resolve itself. If I justify myself and refuse to reconcile, I grow more and more miserable and open myself to demonic influence.

Don't entertain the thought that you are invincible and can never make a mistake. We all have areas in which we are weak, and the wise person knows that. The devil, however, is the epitome of pride, and he will always try to convince you that your problem is somebody else's fault—not yours. He doesn't want you to humble yourself and reconcile; he wants you puffed up, defending your territory at all costs. That way he can retain legal access to your life.

The two little words *I'm sorry* will go a long way toward breaking the devil's hold in a strained relationship. A genuine apology can stop a problem from spiraling out of control, but it takes humility to do it when everything in you wants to blame the other person. However, if you'll go to the person and make a specific, genuine apology and then ask for forgiveness, you'll find the walls of resistance toppling. Not only will you render the devil powerless, but you'll also be genuinely reconciled with that person.

From the time of Adam and Eve's sin, God has always covered His people. He covered Adam and Eve with skins, and He covers our sins by the perfect sacrifice of His Son. When we worship Him for who He is, He covers us in His shadow. When we submit our bodies, minds, and spirits to Him, He covers us through our obedience. When we align our families in clearly defined roles as outlined in the Word of God, He covers us through the protection of divine order. When we walk in love and forgiveness, He keeps us covered from all the devil's attacks to divide and conquer. And when we humble ourselves and confess our sins, He is faithful to forgive and place us once more under His divine covering. That's where I want to dwell. What about you?

Chapter 5

The Three Banners of Battle

Some Christians have the mistaken idea that if they live right, they will never experience any attacks from the devil. They look at those who are struggling and think, "I wonder what they did wrong. I wonder what sin they committed." That's how Job's friends were, and it's easy to develop that kind of self-righteous, smug attitude. If facing a battle meant you were out of the will of God, then Paul spent most of his life out of the will of God. That, we know, was not true, and neither is it true for you.

Being in a battle doesn't necessarily mean you are out of the will of God. It's what you do in the battle that counts, not the fact that you are in the battle to begin with. As we've already mentioned, Psalm 18:34 says that God teaches our hands to war and says we are strong enough to break a bow of steel. Some of us, unfortunately, can't even break a wet spaghetti noodle, much less a steel bow, but if we are teachable, God can show us how to become strong and win in any battle.

I once heard a pastor describe how he came to understand this truth from Psalm 18. Verse 33 in the King James Version of the Bible says, "He maketh my feet like hinds' feet, and setteth me upon my high places." A hind is a certain kind of deer, and this pastor visited a zoo that had these deer living in a setting similar to their natural habitat. In this area was a man-made mountain for the deer to climb, and he couldn't help but notice how nimble and sure-footed the little animals were.

As he observed the deer, two of them on the top of the mountain got into a tussle, and one of the deer lost its balance and began to fall. Much to the pastor's amazement and relief, the hind landed on its feet and immediately darted up the mountain again. In that moment, God spoke to this pastor's heart and said, "If I make your feet like hinds' feet, then the devil might knock you around a little bit, but you're going to land on your feet. And once you land on your feet, you're going right back up the mountain." That is the voice of victory, and that is your destiny as a child of God.

"Though a righteous man falls seven times, he rises again," says Proverbs 24:16 NIV. Never look at how many battles you have fought and maybe even lost, but look at whether you are getting back up again. You might fall . . . and fall . . . and fall, but just get back up. When the snake bites you on the hand (like it did to Paul in Acts 28:3–5), just shake it off. You can be a victor in any battle as long as you get back up again.

In this chapter, I want to show you how to actually engage the enemy in spiritual warfare. As discussed in the previous two chapters, staying under God's covering is more of a defensive strategy, and it will probably occupy the bulk of your time. But there comes a time in every soldier's career when he has to surge forward in attack mode. He does not shed his covering at that time, but he does go on the offensive against the enemy. Like that soldier, you are going to have to learn how to launch an offensive in spiritual warfare.

Have you ever seen one of those old war movies where the two sides line up on opposite sides of a field and when a bugle sounds, they rush madly toward each other? You will notice that there is always a designated person who goes first in battle, carrying a banner that serves as a point of reference for the rest of the troops. That banner has great significance, and seeing it precede them into battle gives the soldiers that extra boost to surge forward and conquer.

When you step forward to engage in spiritual warfare — when you are on one side of the field and the enemy is on the other — God has three banners for you to carry into battle. Under these three banners, you find refuge, courage, and direction. These are the banners of the Lord that propel you to victory.

The Banner of Righteousness: The Blood of Jesus

Second Corinthians 10:3 says, "For though we walk in the flesh, we do not war according to the flesh." In the Bible, the word *flesh* generally refers to our lower nature, our self-centered, natural tendencies. It includes our inclination to depend upon our own abilities and efforts rather than on God. That is the flesh, and it is constantly warring to pull us away from God and His ways.

Following the flesh never brings victory in battle. "For if you live according to the flesh you will die; but if by the Spirit you put to death the deeds of the body, you will live" (Rom 8:13). You cannot war against the devil if you are yet unredeemed and still living in the flesh. You do not have power over the devil when he still has power over you! You are either under the dominion of God, submitted to Him and walking in Christ's righteousness, or you are under the dominion of the devil, with no right to tell him what to do.

The first banner, therefore, that you carry into spiritual battle is the banner of your righteousness in Christ won by His blood shed on the cross. There is no middle ground when it comes to righteousness, no neutral ground where you can claim partial righteousness. You're either righteous or unrighteous—that's it. In fact, 2 Corinthians 6:14 says that righteousness and unrighteousness have nothing in common; they are diametrically opposed to each other. If you are righteous, you will one day live with God in heaven; but if you are unrighteous, you will be condemned to an eternity in hell with the devil. It all depends on your righteousness.

Verse 14 continues with a comparison between light and darkness as representative of righteousness and unrighteousness. When you are righteous, you are full of light spiritually, and no devil can occupy you. When you are unrighteous, the darkness in your spirit is like a magnet for every demon imaginable. You can walk out of the light and into darkness if you so choose, but then you open yourself to the influence of the devil. That's why sin is so awful; not only is it an affront to God, but it also breaches the covering around you and makes it easier for the devil to gain a foothold.

I like the way the late Lester Sumrall explained it. Referring to the borders that separate two opposing countries, he explained that as long as you stay on your side of the border in the land of your birth, you are fine. You enjoy all the rights and privileges that your country offers. However, if you decide one day that you want to cross over the border into the enemy's territory, you will soon find a gun pointed at your head and a prison door clanging behind you. When you willfully step over into the enemy's territory, you have to play by his rules because he's in charge in his country.

Back in 2 Corinthians 6, we read in verse 15, "And what accord has Christ with Belial?" Belial refers to Satan and translated means "lord of the flies." What an apt description of the devil. He's nothing more than a nasty, dirty, disease-carrying pest! When you have the righteousness of Christ covering your heart, you have absolutely nothing in common with the devil. His world and yours are direct opposites.

When you get saved, the blood of Jesus is applied to your heart and life, much like the blood of the Passover lamb was applied to the doorposts of God's people. Then when the devil attacks, you are safe because of the blood of Jesus. The blood applied to your heart says you are God's property and denies the devil the right of access. The blood speaks of the awful price paid for your righteousness. Because that price has already been paid, the enemy has no right to reclaim you for his kingdom. You are righteous and in right standing with God.

If you don't understand how totally complete your righteousness is, the devil will be able to cause you to doubt it. People sometimes come up to me and say they're under condemnation for a particular sin. For some reason, they feel that that one sin is just too terrible to forgive. At times like that, I gently point out to them that God's forgiveness doesn't work that way. You're either forgiven or unforgiven. You're either righteous or unrighteous. You're either light or dark. You can't be declared righteous in some things and unrighteous in others. God doesn't select certain sins to forgive and others to retain. Second Corinthians 5:21 NIV states, "God made him who had no sin to be sin for us, so that in him we might become the righteousness of God." So when you are *in* Christ, covered by his blood, you are righteous. That's it—pure and simple!

This is so important to remember in spiritual warfare because as soon as you start aggressively attacking the devil, he'll counterattack by taking a jab at your righteousness. The minute you say, "Satan, I come against you in the name of Jesus," he shoots a fiery dart back at you. "What about that affair you had three years ago?" he hisses. "You have no right to ask God for anything; you're not worthy."

You have a choice when that happens. You can hang your head and answer, "Yes, you're right. Maybe one of these days I'll feel forgiven, but for now, I'll just go sit in this corner and hide." Or, you can rise up and say, "Yes, you're right; I'm not righteous. But the Bible says that God made Him who had no sin to be sin for me that I might become the righteousness of God. Therefore, I *am* righteous in Christ. Now, scat!"

When you are secure in your righteousness, you have boldness and "confidence to enter the Most Holy Place by the blood of Jesus" (Heb. 10:19 NIV). You know your position is secure, not because of anything you've done, but because of everything Christ has done. That is the basis of your boast—Christ and Christ alone.

Second Corinthians 6:7 NLT says, "God's power has been working in us. We have righteousness as our weapon, both to attack and to defend ourselves." Your righteousness in Christ is your weapon, both offensively and defensively, or as the New King James puts it, you have the "armor of righteousness on the right hand and on the left." In other words, you're totally covered. From every angle and every direction, Christ's righteousness covers you, and you can use that as a weapon.

The devil acts as a prosecuting attorney against God's children. Scripture calls him the accuser of the brethren (Rev. 12:10). He constantly brings up your faults, weaknesses, and failings. But you are not powerless against him; you overcome him with the blood of the Lamb and the word of your testimony (v. 11). Those are your weapons when you know the covering your righteousness in Christ brings.

The Banner of Power: The Name of Jesus

The power of God, which is released through the authority in Jesus' name, is the second banner under which we go into spiritual battle. God's power is all wrapped up in the name of Jesus. When we use that lovely name, we remind the devil of his defeat more than two thousand years ago.

From the earliest days, the power in Jesus' name has long been a part of the Christian experience. The apostles and early disciples knew this and exercised their authority in it. In Ephesians 1:21, Paul tells us that the name of Jesus is "far above all principality and power and might and dominion, and every name that is named, not only in this age but also in that which is to come." Philippians 2:9–10 repeats this, telling us that God has given Jesus "the name which is above every name, that at the name of Jesus every knee should bow, of those in heaven, and of those on earth, and of those under the earth." The name of Jesus is supreme and full of dynamic power.

There's something so significant about a name. When my wife and I got married, she legally took my last name as hers. I know some people today don't think that's necessary; nevertheless, that's what we did, and I still think it's a good idea. Up until the moment we exchanged our vows, however, she was still Melanie Clark and I was still Larry Stockstill, two separate individuals. She had her stuff, and I had mine.

Coming into the marriage, I was the proud owner of a 1971 yellow Javelin with windows that *almost* rolled up. It was mine, flaws and all, and did not belong to Melanie. All that changed, however, the moment we signed the marriage license. All of a sudden, she was Melanie Stockstill, and with the assumption of my name, she had access to everything I owned. Her old name was gone, and now she could take the keys and drive my Javelin anytime she wanted. When she took my name, she got everything that went with it. Full, equal privileges were hers because now she was Melanie Stockstill, not Melanie Clark. That's how it is with a name.

We find in the book of Acts several stories about the power in Jesus' name. One of them is found in the nineteenth chapter. Beginning in verse 12, we see how God used Paul mightily, even to the point where handkerchiefs that he had touched brought healing or deliverance. Observing his power, some itinerant Jewish exorcists thought they could imitate Paul and attain the same results. These men tried to cast out demons by saying, "In the name of Jesus, whom Paul preaches, I command you to come out" (v. 13 NIV). They thought they had stumbled upon a nifty little secret that would give them power: Say the name of Jesus and watch the demons flee!

A priest named Sceva had seven sons, and they were among those using this "magical" formula to call out demon spirits. The problem was, they had no relationship with Jesus, and the demons knew it. On one occasion when they recited their memorized formula, the demon in the man they were trying to deliver challenged them. The spirit boasted, "Jesus I know, and Paul I know; but who are you?" (v. 15). Then the demon physically attacked them, stripping them naked and severely injuring all seven of them (v. 16)!

Notice in this story (which took place in Ephesus, not Israel) that the demon knew exactly who Jesus was. Even though the demon-possessed man lived in a land many miles from where Jesus had ministered, the demon in him knew exactly who Jesus was. Furthermore, the demon knew who Paul was and that Paul was in relationship with Jesus. That's where Paul derived his power: from his relationship with Jesus that gave him the right to use His name. Paul was "married" to Jesus, we could say, and thus was entitled to all the rights of the one whose name he had assumed.

Another story about the power in Jesus' name is found in Acts 16. In this account, a young slave girl following Paul kept exclaiming, "These men are the servants of the Most High God, who proclaim to us the way of salvation" (v. 17). At first thought, that might seem like a good thing; here was a young girl telling everybody what a wonderful minister of the Gospel Paul was. But the girl was possessed with a spirit of divination, and her masters used this to make money. Although her words were true, their source was evil.

Just because something sounds right, looks right, or makes you feel goose bumps doesn't mean it's from God. If someone can talk the talk but doesn't walk the walk, pay no attention to what he says. Discern the source and judge from that.

The Bible says that's what Paul did. "But Paul, greatly annoyed, turned and said to the spirit, 'I command you in the name of Jesus Christ to come out of her' " (v. 18). He was not fooled or flattered by this spirit that seemingly wanted to say good things about him. He refused to have dealings with anything that was impure and of a different spirit than the Holy Spirit.

Remember that when you hear someone speaking in the name of Jesus who says she can read your palm. Remember that when someone offers to give you a personal prophecy while you pray with her in a secret room full of candles. That's a spirit of divination in action; have nothing to do with it.

When Paul took authority over the spirit of divination, it was quite a simple affair. He made a brief, to-the-point statement: "I command you in the name of Jesus Christ to come out of her." He used the name of Jesus, spoke it aloud, and the desired result manifested.

Some people think getting demons to leave is a hard task that only special people and specific actions can accomplish. Paul made it simple, and so should we. You don't have to rub somebody bald or stroke his throat or repeat phrases over and over until the wee hours of the morning. You've got to know the authority you have in the name of Jesus and use it. Of course, the Holy Spirit may lead you to do certain things, and you certainly can't put a time limit on ministry, but the point is, the authority is in the name you use and your right to use it as a child of God.

The Banner of Truth: The Word of God

The third banner of battle is the truth we have in the Word of God. In every way, the devil is the antithesis of God. God is good; the devil is bad. God is merciful; the devil is merciless. God is truth; the devil has no truth within him. In describing the devil, the Bible says that he "has always hated the truth. . . . When he lies, it is consistent with his character; for he is a liar and the father of lies" (John 8:44 NLT).

When you fight against the devil, you've got to stay in bounds by fighting him in scriptural ways. If you go outside the bounds of Scripture, you can get into some really goofy and downright dangerous ways of dealing with the devil. Some people have come up with all kinds of far-out methods to wage spiritual warfare instead of sticking with what the Bible clearly teaches. Prayer, fasting, the blood of Jesus, the name of Jesus, and the Word of God are all legitimate spiritual weapons found and explained within the Bible.

The devil will always try to move you outside the realm of the Scriptures. He did that with Eve. "Did God really say, 'You must not eat from any tree in the garden'?" he said in Genesis 3:1 NIV. Eve couldn't be tricked at this point, answering correctly, "We may eat fruit from the trees in the garden" (v. 2), but then she deviated from what God had really said. She continued, "But God did say, 'You must not eat fruit from the tree that is in the middle of the garden, and *you must not touch it,* or you will die' " (v. 3, emphasis added).

If you look back in Genesis 2:16–17, you will see that God did command Adam and Eve not to eat from one certain tree, but He never said anything about touching it. That was Eve's addition to God's words. Satan subverted the truth, and when Eve listened to him, she ended up subverting the truth of God's words even more.

Deception is one of the devil's primary weapons. He used it against Eve, and he even tried to use it against Jesus. When

Jesus fasted in the desert, Satan attacked Him three times, and each time he twisted the Word of God in an attempt to cause Jesus to sin. Jesus, of course, was well aware of the devil's tactics and countered with the true intent of God's holy Word.

Jesus wielded the pure, unadulterated Word of God as a formidable weapon against Satan's lies, and you have that same powerful privilege. In whatever area you are battling the devil, you've got to find the truth that the Word of God says about it and then use that as a weapon against the devil. He cannot prevail against the truth.

A woman in our church was once told that she could not have children apart from medical intervention. She did first try what medicine had to offer, but it was to no avail. She then decided she would go to the Word of God and find Scriptures about having children. She did this and put these verses on cards tacked up all around her house—in the kitchen, in the bathroom, everywhere. She kept the Word of God in front of her and meditated on it constantly, and sure enough, she conceived and had a child. Not only did she do this once, but she did it again and had another child! I dedicated both those children to the Lord. They were the fruit of her victory in carrying the Word of God as a banner against the enemy.

The promises in the Word of God are truth and reality. Outward circumstances are irrelevant. Even if it seems as though you are making no progress, keep picking up your sword and slashing at the enemy. Every time you speak the truth of Scripture, you're cutting the devil down to size. He hates for you to speak the Word because he knows it's true.

When he tells you, "You're going bankrupt," you can answer, "No, I'm blessed in the city and blessed in the field. The windows of heaven are open, and God is pouring out a blessing." Keep pointing the sword at him, needling him with it.

When the devil tells you, "You'll never get well; you'll always be sick and in pain," pick up your sword and say, "By His stripes, I am healed." Keep the Word of God flowing. From whatever direction the enemy attacks, just whirl around and give him the point of the sword. Keep pivoting and lunging until finally you go in for the kill. That's how you fight the devil, and that's how you defeat him.

If you're like most Christians, you probably have several Bibles lying around your house. They may be quite expensive and quite beautiful. If that's as far as you ever go—just admiring how beautiful your Bible is, but never opening it and reading it—the devil isn't the least bit threatened. What he doesn't want is for you to know the truth that's in it and to pick it up, point it at him, and say, "Back up!"

Your Bible is your sword. Bringing it to church a couple of times a week and then leaving it on your bookshelf the rest of the week is not going to cut it. It's truth, life, and power. It's life-changing, earth-shaking, and world-transforming. It's a mighty banner, and with it you can run boldly into the fray of battle, confident of victory.

Never forget that God goes before you in every spiritual battle. You face nothing alone but carry His righteousness, name, and Word with you. Covered in His blood, you possess His righteousness. Using His name, you unleash His power. Embracing His Word, you declare His truth against every enemy. These three banners declare you worthy, competent, bold, and fearless. They are the banners of war, and they are the banners of victory.

Chapter 6

Levels and Areas of Demonic Activity

There are four levels of demonic attack. Each of these begins in the realm of the mind, or the thought life. If you permit him, the devil will move from one level to the next to the degree to which you tolerate his actions. Within these four levels, he attacks in many varied forms, but all these forms can be grouped into nine very broad categories. Let's look first at the levels of attack and then proceed to the nine specific areas in which the enemy strikes.

Level 1: Imaginations

The key to understanding demonic attack is found in 2 Corinthians 10:5. The King James Version of this verse reads, "Casting down imaginations, and every high thing that exalteth itself against the knowledge of God, and bringing into captivity every thought to the obedience of Christ." Thoughts occur in the realm of the mind, or soul, and this is where the real battles of your life are waged. The mind is the place where "the rubber meets the road."

The mind is the place from which sin proceeds. You don't wake up one day and decide to commit adultery or some other sin. It is a process that begins with a thought that eventually leads to an action if allowed to go unchecked. The apostle James explained it this way: "Temptation comes from the lure of our own evil desires. These evil desires lead to evil actions, and evil actions lead to death" (James 1:14–15 NLT).

When the devil initiates his attack, he begins very subtly by first interjecting a thought into your mind. This is what we mean by the word *imaginations*. Some translations use the words *speculations, reasonings,* or *suggestions*. That's precisely what the devil does when he attacks at this first level.

One day as you're walking along praising God for His goodness, a thought suddenly comes into your mind that is totally foreign to you: "Why don't you turn into that adult bookstore for a minute or two? It won't hurt to see what others struggle with. That way you can minister to them better. It won't affect you." Now you've never gone into an adult bookstore before and never even wanted to, but just as you're walking by that place, this thought pops into your head. That is an "imagination," a "suggestion" that is contrary to God's Word. You don't need to experience what the sinner is struggling with in order to help him; that kind of reasoning comes from the devil, not God.

I have learned to immediately compare any thought with the truth of God's Word. If it lines up, then I know it's from Him. If it doesn't, I discard it. Make it a practice to do that and you'll stop many a wrong thought dead in its tracks.

It's easy, however, to be led astray by the devil if you're not aware of how he attacks. If you don't realize that he tries to infiltrate your mind, you won't recognize his attacks. You'll accept his thoughts as your own, ignorant to their true source. That's what happened to Eve in the Garden of Eden. Paul, speaking to the Corinthians, said, "As the serpent deceived

Eve by his craftiness, so your minds may be corrupted from the simplicity that is in Christ" (2 Cor. 11:3).

Believing the devil's lies, Eve left the simplicity of following God and listened to the enemy. This is recorded in Genesis 3. In verse 1 NIV we read, "Now the serpent was more crafty than any of the wild animals the Lord God had made. He said to the woman, 'Did God really say, "You must not eat from any tree in the garden"?' " He came to Eve with a question, with an innocent-sounding comment: "Did God really say?" He was trying to put just the tiniest shadow of doubt in Eve's mind as to what God had really said. *Maybe you misunderstood, Eve. Maybe you just think that's what God said. Maybe you weren't really paying attention.* He started with just a subtle thought.

At first Eve handled the serpent just fine. She corrected him and said that she and Adam could eat from all the trees except one. If Eve had stopped right there, she would have been fine. She was not entertaining the devil's thought and was clear in God's word to her. If she had terminated the conversation right then, the entire course of human history might have been different. But she kept talking with the devil.

Sometimes we think that if we had been the one in the Garden, we would have never fallen for Satan's tricks, but I don't think that's true. We do it every day—bat the ball back and forth with the devil in the recesses of our minds. He comes with a thought and lobs it our way, like in a game of tennis, and we keep lobbing the ball back and forth with him instead of walking off the court in the beginning of the contest.

So Eve lobbed the ball back to the serpent. When he sent it back the next time, he hit it harder. *Well, Eve, if you eat the fruit, you'll become as wise as God.* Eve was definitely interested in the game by now. Maybe she thought, *Yes, it is the tree of the knowledge of good and evil. If I eat it, I will be wise. I'm sure God would want me to be wise. Then we would have so much more in common.*

When you keep playing tennis with the devil, he is going to win. You're not good enough, smart enough, or talented enough to best him. He's the master at the game, and he is content with nothing less than total victory. You are the prize.

The best thing you can do when the devil tries to engage you in a tennis match is to slam the first ball back with a Holy Ghost forehand and then head for the showers! Walk off the court and don't look back. Don't think you are such a mighty athlete that you can just keep the game going for a while. End it quick!

If you stop the game here, you've stopped that imagination, that vain thought, from progressing. You've stopped it cold before it has a chance to plant itself in your mind. That's the first and most important step in defeating the devil.

Level 2: High Thoughts

Unfortunately, we don't always stop imaginations when they come into our minds. Maybe we don't recognize them or don't really understand how dangerous they are, but nevertheless, we move to the next level, the level of high thoughts. This happens when we start meditating on the thought the devil has placed in our mind. This is what Eve did. The devil said, "Did God really say?" and she first answered, "Yes, He said." Then the devil replied, "God doesn't want you to be wise like Him," and she started thinking about it and turning it over in her mind.

"The woman saw that the tree was good for food. . . ." (v. 6). The woman should have just turned her back on the tree and walked away from it. She would have been free and so would the entire human race have remained free. Instead, she looked at the tree; she gazed upon it and kept staring at it, thinking about how good its fruit would taste. *What could really be wrong with just a little taste? God made it good for food.* That was Eve's first justification, and it's the same one we use: *What would it hurt if I . . .?*

". . . It was pleasant to the eyes. . . ." (v. 6). Now Eve's thoughts began pulling her further and further from God's words. *The fruit is so beautiful! Nothing that beautiful could be bad.* That's exactly what the devil wanted her to think, and he'll try to use that same trick on you. But everything that glitters is not gold, as the old saying goes. The devil is a master at making sin and evil look beautiful and enticing. It's one of the premier tricks of his trade.

". . . A tree desirable to make one wise . . ." (v. 6). That was the clincher for Eve. *Everyone needs more wisdom. I'll be able to follow God better. I'll be a better person.* And with that final thought, she stretched forth her hand, and "she took of its fruit and ate. She also gave to her husband with her, and he ate" (v. 6). She stepped across the boundary God had set, committed the act, and even involved Adam in it. With that chain of events, sin entered the human race.

Level 3: Strongholds

When Eve took the fruit and ate it, she moved toward the third level of demonic attack. When your imagination becomes a high thought that leads to an action, you have entered a realm where a stronghold can become entrenched. I'm not saying that every time you sin you erect a stronghold, but I'm saying that when you consciously sin, it becomes easier to sin in that area the next time . . . and the next time . . . and the next time. Unrepented, habitual sin can then lead to the establishment of a stronghold in your mind. Satan now has access to this area of your life, and you find it very difficult to resist him. It becomes a pattern of behavior, a habit that is extremely difficult to overcome.

That's why you can't fool around with sin. When you know you've done something wrong, be quick to confess it and repent of it. Don't excuse yourself or rationalize what you have done or why you have done it. Just repent! That way you quickly close the door on the devil and keep him from being able to set up shop in your mind or body and torment you with an ongoing problem, fear, or sin.

You can have a stronghold in one area or several. You can recognize its presence by the fact that it is an area of your life in which you sense a lack of control or victory. Although you may experience victory in other areas, you find this particular area especially difficult. And it all started with an unchecked thought that led to a sinful action that became a pattern that resulted in bondage.

Level 4: Possession

There's a big difference between oppression and possession. I personally do not believe a Christian can be possessed by the devil, but I do believe he can be oppressed. A believer's spirit has been claimed for the kingdom of God, and the Holy Spirit lives inside every genuinely born-again person. Darkness cannot cohabit with light, and the Holy Spirit will not cohabit with the devil. Nevertheless, if a believer consistently yields an area of his life to sin, he can allow the devil entrance to that part of his life and be oppressed in that area. That is oppression—not possession.

Possession occurs in someone who does not know Christ who has yielded himself to demonic control. At this stage, the evil spirit has merged with the person's personality and taken control of the individual. The person can no longer exercise free will; he is under the control of the demon. He may be insane and out of touch with reality. This possession occurs at the deepest level of the person's spirit.

You may not ever encounter a truly demon-possessed person, but in some parts of the world, this is much more common than in the United States. You do, however, need to be aware of the four levels the devil moves through when trying to attack your life: imaginations, high thoughts, strongholds, and possession. He will go as far as you will let him go. His goal never changes: to steal, kill, and destroy and take you to hell with him.

Nine Areas of Demonic Activity

When the devil is operating at some level in a person's life, he will usually manifest in a particular way. There are many different kinds of demons, but I believe that the Scriptures identify nine major spirits under which we could group all other demons. I want to take them one at a time and show you how they work in a person's life.

You do not have to live under the oppression of a demonic influence. Galatians 5:1 says, "Stand fast therefore in the liberty by which Christ has made us free, and do not be entangled again with a yoke of bondage." In other words, it is possible to have been free in Christ and then walk again in bondage to the devil. That's what happens when you start entertaining imaginations and high thoughts.

Continuing in verse 13, the Bible says, "For you, brethren, have been called to liberty." Freedom is what the Gospel is all about—freedom from sin, sickness, bondage, and oppression. God doesn't want you living under the influence of demon spirits, but in the joy and freedom of the Holy Spirit.

Verses 16–17 tell us how to walk in this freedom: "Walk in the Spirit, and you shall not fulfill the lust of the flesh. For the flesh lusts against the Spirit, and the Spirit against the flesh; and these are contrary to one another, so that you do not do the things that you wish." Living and walking in the power of the Spirit of God is the key to living victoriously over the devil. A constant tug-of-war exists between your flesh and the Spirit within you. It's only as you learn to rely upon and release the Spirit that you will find the ability to war against and overcome the devil.

Verses 19–21 list the works of the flesh that will take root in your life if you don't learn how to take authority over them. I believe they can be grouped into nine broad categories that show areas in which the devil attacks and tries to gain strongholds. The first of these is fear.

Spirit of Fear

Although many people struggle with fear, it is contrary to the Word of God. "For you did not receive the spirit of bondage again to fear, but you received the Spirit of adoption by whom we cry out, 'Abba, Father' " (Rom. 8:15). Your security in your position as a child of God is the greatest tool you have to combat fear. As you grow in maturity and awareness of your position in Christ, fear should be exerting less influence over you. If that is not the case, perhaps you are not recognizing it when it comes.

Simply put, fear is the feeling you get when Satan places before your mind events that haven't even happened and most probably never will! Maybe you wake up at night and your teenaged son isn't home yet, and the thought courses through your mind that maybe he was in a terrible automobile accident. You think you're just being a concerned parent by thinking that, but really the devil is planting that thought there. The more you entertain the thought, the more fearful you become, until finally you are up pacing the floor and frantically calling your child's cell phone. When he doesn't answer, you become more convinced than ever that something terrible has happened. By the time your child walks casually through the door, you are in a heap on the floor, crying and carrying on for fear of all the horrible things that might have happened to him. Your son looks at you like you are crazy and calmly explains that he locked himself out of his car and hadn't taken his cell phone with him so couldn't call you. It just took him a little longer than usual to get home, but you were convinced that he was lying dead in a ditch or unidentified in some intensive care unit. That's how far unrestrained fear will take you.

Fear is a progression. It starts with a thought: "I wonder if they caught that guy who was breaking into homes in our city?" If you don't rebuke it right there, it grows: "I heard he was in our neighborhood last week." At every point in the process, you can shut down the "tennis game" or keep lobbing the ball back and forth with the devil. You don't even realize what you're doing, but each thought gets worse than the one before it. "Did I lock the door tonight?" becomes "I hear someone pulling on the door!" and finally you're trembling, sweating, and reaching for the phone to call 911!

A fear unchecked becomes a bondage, and if you repeat that pattern of behavior often enough, it can become a stronghold in your life. You might be fearful of disease, accidents, financial bankruptcy, divorce, wayward children, or any number or combination of things, but the end result is a sick feeling in the pit of your stomach that something terrible is going to happen to you or someone you love. After a while, you find it harder and harder to resist; you live with it, day after day and year after year. You quit trying to use the Word of God against it; you tolerate it and it becomes a stronghold in your life.

Brothers and sisters, you don't have to live like that. Second Timothy 1:7 really is true! God has not given you "a spirit of fear, but of power and of love and of a sound mind." Begin meditating on the truth of the power, love, and sound mind inside of you, especially when fear comes knocking at the door. The Holy Spirit lives in you, and that Spirit is greater than any demon from hell that comes against you. Begin training your mind to think on how powerful God's Spirit is on the inside of you.

As you find faith arising, move to meditating on God's love. The Bible says, "Perfect love casts out fear" (1 John

4:18). The more you think on God's love, the less time you have to think on fear. The more you meditate on the fact that God loves you and is in control of every aspect of your life, the more you can trust Him. Just as thinking fearful thoughts can pull you further and further into bondage, thinking about God's power and love will consistently pull your thoughts upward to Him.

Finally, declare that in Christ you have a sound mind. That means a disciplined mind, a mind whose thoughts are under control. Some of us, though, have flabby minds that are out of shape through lack of discipline. We've let any and every thought imaginable take up residence in our minds. We've become lazy, not wanting to work at renewing our minds with God's Word. Whenever a fearful thought comes into our minds, we are so spiritually weak and flabby that we don't even have the strength to rebuke the devil and go about our business.

Fear is not usually very rational. That's because it's based on a "what if" instead of a "what is." Some people, for example, are afraid of water, so much so that they fear getting water baptized. That, of course, is not a rational fear. To my knowledge, no pastor has ever lost a believer in the baptismal waters, but the devil tells you that you'll be the first! He tells you the pastor is too skinny and can't possibly pull you out of the water. He tells you you're going to inhale while under the water and choke to death. He'll tell you anything—it doesn't have to be rational—to get you to fear and not trust God.

You don't have to embrace those kinds of thoughts. You don't have to dance with the devil. Take the Holy Ghost as your partner, and at the first hint of a fearful thought, take authority over it. Say, "Oh, no, devil. I'm not going to drown in the baptismal pool. God goes with me, wherever I go. The blood of Jesus covers me, and the perfect love of the Holy Ghost in me is casting out all fear." Then get on down to the church and follow the Lord in water baptism!

Spirit of Heaviness

The second area in which demons attack is depression, or a "spirit of heaviness" (Isa. 61:3). This refers to sadness, sorrow, despair, and hopelessness. It grows, just like fear does, when you receive an imagination and let it become a high thought. You might wake up one morning and feel a little blue—no particular reason for it, but you just don't feel like your normal self. You look at your spouse lying there beside you and decide that she is the reason for your blahs. "She sure doesn't look like she used to. And she never gets up and fixes my breakfast for me anymore," a husband might think. If he continues with that line of thought, he'll soon magnify it from "I'm feeling a little down today" to "I've never been happy while married to this woman." Then he starts thinking of all the people he's ever known who got divorced and decides that's his destiny too.

All this process might take a while to go through his mind, but the point is, if he entertains thoughts of how unfulfilling and depressing his marriage is, sooner or later he begins despairing of its ever getting better. Then he's just one step away from hopelessness. In extreme cases, hopelessness can lead a person to make the decision to end it all rather than endure any more agony.

People who commit suicide have lost all hope. They can no longer see any possible solution for their problems and somehow feel that even God cannot help. They come to a totally false conclusion about their lives and believe the devil's lie that the only solution is to kill themselves.

I truly feel for those caught in such a hopeless trap, and I have had some firsthand experience with it. I know the despair that drives a person to that point, and I know the repercussions of the terrible act, but I also believe that it begins with a thought. If not checked, these thoughts lead to a spirit of heaviness descending upon the person. It is a spirit every bit as real and even more destructive than the spirit of fear.

Isaiah 61:3 gives the antidote to depression and hopelessness: "the garment of praise for the spirit of heaviness." All of us experience ups and downs in our emotions, but a Spirit-filled person has the Word of God and the Holy Spirit to help him maintain emotional and mental equilibrium. He has the privilege of offering praise to God in any and every situation, and this, I believe, is the key to overcoming depression. When you consciously choose to praise, you refute every lie of the devil and replace negative, hopeless thoughts with the truth found in God's Word.

There is hope in every situation; nothing is beyond the touch of God. But you've got to control your mind and train your thoughts to know that. Isaiah 35:10 NLT says, "Those who have been ransomed by the Lord will return to Jerusalem, singing songs of everlasting joy. Sorrow and mourning will disappear, and they will be *overcome* with joy and gladness" (emphasis added). When you're tempted to despair, return to the Lord and sing joyfully before Him. As you continue to proclaim His greatness and your trust in His power, you will be overcome with joy.

Every day I bind sorrow and sadness off my life. I loose everlasting joy to be upon me, and when the devil sends a discouraging thought my way, I start singing a song to the Lord. When I fix my eyes upon Him and release praise from my heart, I defeat the devil and soon find peace and joy returning, or "overcoming" me. If you'll do that and be consistent in it, you'll find your times of depression getting less and less frequent and hope becoming a dominant feature in your life.

Spirit of Jealousy

Numbers 5:14 NKJV speaks about a spirit of jealousy in connection with a man who suspects his wife of adultery, but it could apply to any other area of life as well. It is basically an imagination that someone else is a threat to your life, success, or happiness.

No person is a threat to your success. In God's economy, the blessing of one does not diminish the blessing of another. He does indeed want to bless and prosper you, but He does not have to eliminate other people in order for you to succeed. His goodness and potential to bless are limitless, so someone else's success has nothing to do with yours.

If you can keep that fact firmly planted in your mind, you'll be okay, but the devil will never be content to leave you alone. He'll try to persuade you that a particular person is the only one standing between you and your perceived success or good fortune. "If he didn't work here, I just know I would have been the one to get the big promotion," you stew. Or, "If she hadn't been around, then 'Mr. Right' would have asked me out," you fume.

You can always find someone who has something you don't. Someone else will always seem to have more money, more friends, more prestige, or more blessing than you. If you dwell on that, a spirit of jealousy begins to grow inside of you. The more you think about how much the other person seems to have, the more you feel cheated in your own life. It just doesn't seem fair, and you grow more and more disgruntled and unhappy.

When you find yourself feeling jealous, stop and ask yourself, "Who is in control of my life?" If you say that God is, then recognize His hand in the circumstances that come your way and rejoice in that. If "Mr. Right" chooses someone else, accept it, because it just means God has selected someone else for you. If your coworker gets the promotion, hallelujah!—that just means there's something better for you down the road. Their blessing has nothing to do with you, and that realization will cause you to truly rejoice and be happy when others get blessed. Your time is coming, if you'll be happy for others, wait on God for your blessing, and refuse to allow jealousy entrance into your heart.

Spirit of Anger

There is often a correlation between the various areas of demonic attack. Opening the door in one area can lead to oppression in another area as well. This was quite obvious in King Saul's life. As you remember, when God rejected him as king, Saul became oppressed with a tormenting spirit that only David's harp playing could soothe. First Samuel 16:14 NLT describes the spirit in these terms: "a tormenting spirit that filled him with depression and fear."

In 1 Samuel 18, when David returned after killing Goliath, the women began to sing about the ten thousands he had slain in comparison to Saul's thousands. Verses 8 and 9 in the NIV say, "Saul was very angry; this refrain galled him. 'They have credited David with tens of thousands,' he thought, 'but me with only thousands. What more can he get but the kingdom?' And from that time on Saul kept a jealous eye on David." Saul's depression progressed to jealousy, and then, as we've already discussed, Saul's jealousy turned into anger and hatred so strong that he tried to take David's life several times.

That's why all these areas of demonic attack are so dangerous. Entertaining one leads to entertaining another, then another, until finally you are doing things you never dreamed possible. You only make the situation much worse by refusing to own up to what's going on in your heart to begin with. That's where it all begins—in the heart. Jesus knew that and told us, "For out of the heart proceed evil thoughts, murders, adulteries, fornications, thefts, false witness, blasphemies" (Matt. 15:19).

When you get angry, don't just gloss over it, saying, "Oh, that's just my Irish temperament," or "I'm just an expressive person." It's not your Irish temperament or expressive personality—it's the spirit of anger trying to take up residence in you. If you'll deal with it immediately, it won't be able to set up house; if you entertain it even a moment, it will not rest until it occupies the entire dwelling.

Anger is so dangerous and can lead to disastrous consequences. I've had men who physically abused their wives tell me they would never have thought they could hurt their wives. But they did. That's how insidious unchecked anger is, and that's why you have to squelch it the minute it raises its ugly head.

Think about it. When your wife forgets to do the laundry, does it really matter? When your husband is late for dinner, does it really matter? When your boss refuses you the raise you deserve, does it really matter? Develop an eternal perspective on life and you'll find there are fewer and fewer things to get angry about. That's how you get delivered from anger.

Spirit of Deception

The fifth spirit is a lying spirit, or a spirit of deception, and it is identified in 2 Chronicles 18:20. The basis for this spirit is pride. People who continually lie want to be someone they are not. They want to project a certain image because they are not secure with the person God made them to be. Because of pride, they want to impress people or be accepted and loved by everyone. They fear rejection, real or perceived, so in an attempt to avoid it, they fabricate lies to present a better picture of themselves. Interestingly, in the process they fool not only others but also themselves.

I've seen this at work. People will eventually believe their own lies. They'll rationalize why they need to lie and then concoct a story to cover all their bases. They begin repeating the lie, and the longer it goes on, the more they actually believe it. Soon the deception is so great they can't even remember the original truth.

Deception is just like any of the other spirits; it starts slowly, a seeming little thing, but it grows by leaps and bounds far beyond its original proportions. This is what happened to Ananias and Sapphira in Acts 5. Ananias and Sapphira were good "church people" who loved God and belonged to the local fellowship. However, the devil played on their pride and told them how to make it look like they were doing something they really weren't.

At the very end of chapter 4 in the book of Acts, Barnabas sold some land and gave all the proceeds to the work of the Lord. The Bible doesn't say so, but I imagine this might have caused quite a stir. It was an exceptionally generous gift, and probably many applauded Barnabas and sang his praises for what he did in purity of heart.

Apparently, Ananias and Sapphira noticed and wanted the same kind of attention. They devised a plan to sell some land and bring a portion of the proceeds to the apostles but claim that it was the full amount. They would have been perfectly justified to give whatever amount they chose, but pride urged them to present a false picture in order to receive the accolades of men.

Peter, however, full of the Holy Spirit, saw right through their tainted scheme and said, "Ananias, why has Satan filled your heart to lie to the Holy Spirit and keep back part of the price of the land for yourself?" (Acts 5:3). He spoke a little more, and then the judgment of God fell, striking Ananias dead. Sapphira arrived three hours later, and when questioned, she repeated the story that she and her husband had fabricated. Her judgment fell just as swiftly, and she was buried alongside her husband (vv. 7–10).

Can you see how serious it is to lie, to get in league with the devil and perpetuate his deception? In God's eyes, it can be a matter of life and death. Stay away from any form of deception. That includes not only blatant, obvious lies, but also any intent to deceive. A lie is anything that is not real and true, anything that is not factual, anything that distorts the full truth. There's no such thing as a little white lie. All lying is wrong because it is prompted by an evil spirit.

When you realize that someone has gotten a wrong impression about you that makes you look better than you really are, clear up the misunderstanding. Don't take credit for what someone else does at work. If the boss thinks you did a wonderful job on a project, but you know that someone else did the bulk of the work, don't smile and say thank you for something someone else did.

Don't exaggerate; that's a form of lying too. Be brutally honest with the truth, and reject deception of any type. Make honesty, openness, and transparency a way of life. In that way, the spirit of deception will have no entrance into your heart.

Spirit of Adultery

This unclean, evil spirit is mentioned in Hosea 4:12 and refers to illicit sexual activity, one of which is adultery. Jesus said that adultery begins by entertaining lust in the heart: "Whoever looks at a woman to lust for her has already committed adultery with her in his heart" (Matt. 5:28). This is not talking about every time a man notices an attractive woman. To simply notice is not sin; it's what you do with it. If you look and keep looking and then start dwelling on all kinds of lustful thoughts that enter your mind, you're opening yourself to the spirit of adultery.

The devil will try to paint your mind with mental pornography (that's what lust is). When sexual images that are ungodly, unbiblical, and outside the realm of marriage race through your mind, you'd better take authority over them. You'd better stop right there and smash the ball to the other side of the court, so to speak. Replace the unclean thought with thoughts about your spouse and how wonderful he or she is. Lift your hands right then and praise God for your partner.

113

When the devil tells you that you got stuck in your marriage, that there's someone smarter and better for you, don't entertain that thought. Remember that he's the father of lies and can speak no truth. He's a liar and is trying to lead you into an affair. Resist him and make up your mind to love and appreciate the spouse God has given you.

If you let your thoughts run rampant, eventually you will give in to the action. I remember Kenneth Hagin talking about this one time, and his example was so sobering I never forgot it. He related the story of a pastor's wife who had left her husband for another man. In a vision, the Lord showed him what had happened in this woman's life and how the devil tries to do the same thing in our lives too.

In the vision, Brother Hagin saw something like a black spot enter the woman's mind and say to her, "Aren't you sad that all your life you've had to live as a pastor's wife? You've missed all the fun in life."

The woman responded, "I rebuke you, Satan," and the spot disappeared. It soon returned, however, and this time she did not reject the evil thought when it came. As she accepted the thought, Brother Hagin saw the spot move from the top of her mind and sink deeper into her. The more the woman gave in to the thought, the deeper it sank into her mind. Ultimately, she completely embraced the thought and agreed with the spirit that spoke it to her. At that point, she ran off with the other man.

Brothers and sisters, you have to be ruthless when dealing with that kind of spirit. You have no concept of the heartache to come if you entertain even one thought of adultery. You have no idea of what you're setting into motion when you start meditating on those kinds of thoughts. Be merciless with any image, mental picture, or thought that makes you think you're not happy with your spouse. Follow the prophet Malachi's advice and guard your spirit so that you will stay loyal and faithful to your spouse (Mal. 2:15).

Spirit of Uncleanness

The next spirit, a spirit of uncleanness, is identified in Mark 1:23. Although all demons are unclean, unholy things, there is a separate class specifically called unclean spirits. This is a broad category, but generally unclean spirits are spirits that mock natural sexual relationships. In addition, there is often a component of idolatrous religious practices associated with them. These unclean spirits are spirits of perversion that focus on unnatural sexual relationships or acts. Incest is such a spirit, and so is homosexuality.

Another unclean spirit is flagrant nakedness. It is not normal behavior to want to publicly exhibit your naked body. Demons drive people to do that, just like they did with the man in Mark 5 who was found "sitting and clothed and in his right mind" after Jesus delivered him. But as long as the unclean spirit was in control, this poor man lived in a cemetery, roaming around screaming and cutting himself—totally insane.

These unclean spirits pervert not only normal sexual relationships but also normal, pure worship of God. Many pagan cultures reflect this relationship between sexual perversion and religious perversion. They seem to go hand in hand, so where you find one, you'll often find the other.

Spirit of Infirmity

Jesus confronted this type of spirit in Luke 13:10 when He healed "a woman who had a spirit of infirmity eighteen years, and was bent over and could in no way raise herself up." She had a condition that sapped her strength and ability to live a life of vitality and vigor.

Now just think for a moment of that woman, so frail and bent over—for eighteen years at the devil's mercy. He had made such an ugly picture of her life. That's how he is and how he always operates. He is ugly, ruthless, and wicked; he will afflict you as long as you will tolerate it.

That's the condition this woman was in until Jesus showed up on the scene. Then everything changed. "When Jesus saw her, He called her to Him and said to her, 'Woman, you are loosed from your infirmity.' And He laid His hands on her, and immediately she was made straight, and glorified God" (vv. 12–13).

Another example of a spirit of infirmity is related in Luke 11:14. This time the spirit manifested as a mute spirit, preventing the person from being able to speak until Jesus cast the spirit out. Just like with the woman, this man's body had been bound from functioning normally by the presence of an evil spirit.

Not every sickness, of course, is caused by a demon, because sometimes we cause our bodies to break down by failing to take proper care of them. Other times we are exposed to certain bacteria or viruses that result in disease. Nevertheless, many times there is a demonic element present in a sickness or chronic condition. It takes wisdom to know when a spirit of infirmity is at work, but God will show you, if you ask.

Personally, I believe that growths are demonic. I believe there is a life-force within a cancer that causes abnormal, unhealthy growth. Only an antilife spirit would nourish something that kills. Nevertheless, you can't make judgments as to why certain people get cancer. That's not a question you need to ask, but you can take authority over the infirm spirit at work and cast it out in the name of Jesus.

Spirits of infirmity come in all shapes and sizes and can attack any part of the human body. Even Spirit-filled Christians are not immune to their attacks. Whenever you notice something in your body that is not quite right, don't just sit back and accept it. Don't say, "Well, I'm just getting older. It's only natural to start having problems." Refuse to tolerate whatever condition pops up in your body, but rather speak against it every day. Don't get weaker; get stronger.

Don't sit down in the fight, but stand. Take dominion over every spirit of infirmity that tries to latch onto your body. It might take a day, it might take a month, or it might take a year; but every spirit of infirmity has to bow to the name of Jesus when you use that mighty weapon day in and day out.

Spirit of Divination

The final spirit I want to mention is the spirit of divination. We see many instances in Scripture in which people performed miracles because of the influence of this kind of spirit. Pharaoh's sorcerers and magicians turned their rods into serpents, just like Moses did (Ex. 7:11–12). In Acts 8, we read about Simon, a very influential sorcerer. Acts 13 chronicles the influence of Elymas, another sorcerer and false prophet. In Acts 16:16, a young slave girl was described as being "possessed with a spirit of divination." There have always been those who can exercise supernatural powers because of their alliance with spirits of divination.

Just because people do miraculous things is no guarantee that what they are doing is from the Lord. Look at the source of their power. Do they profess Christ as Lord? Are they full of the Holy Spirit? Do their lives exhibit Christlikeness? Things are not always what they seem.

Demons of divination are real, and you can't afford to play around with them. Don't fool with anything that is outside the scope of the Bible and the lordship of Christ. You need to keep your surroundings free of any image, statue, painting, or object that represents worship of any god but the one true God. It might be a good idea for you to take a look around your home and see if you have anything that glorifies a false god. If you do, get rid of it. Otherwise, it can give the devil legal access into your life. Throw out the horoscopes, astrology books, tarot cards, or anything else that you think will give you some kind of supernatural insight and power. Give no place to it—you can't afford to.

Sometimes even Spirit-filled Christians fall into the trap of listening to these spirits of divination. They'll visit fortune-tellers, sometimes unaware, since these people often call themselves "prophet" or "prophetess." Those who offer "spiritual" insight for a fee are fortune-tellers, regardless of what they call themselves.

Even though prophecy is a legitimate gift of the Spirit, you have to be careful in this area. I get concerned about Christians who constantly look for someone to prophesy to them. They run searching for prophets, begging, "Give me a word; give me a prophecy; what sayeth the Lord?" That's very, very dangerous, and if you've been guilty of that, you need to repent of it today and start looking to God alone for direction.

Don't believe every spirit; test them, as 1 John 4:1 instructs. Judge with sound judgment, and don't be deceived by outward appearances. Be on guard for false prophets and teachers who seem to have "special" insight.

Fear, heaviness, jealousy, anger, deception, adultery, uncleanness, infirmity, and divination—these are the nine specific spirits that oppress and torment people. As I said, they could be classified differently, but this categorization gives you a good idea of some of the specific ways the devil and his demons will try to infiltrate your life. They enter first at the point of the imagination, hoping to establish a high thought that becomes a stronghold that leads to sinful actions. But thank God, we are not powerless against the enemy's devices. The Word of God tells us what to do.

Overcoming the Enemy

Luke 11:20–22 gives the key to overcoming any attack from the enemy. This passage was spoken by Jesus, and He said, "If I cast out demons with the finger of God, surely the kingdom of God has come upon you. When a strong man, fully armed, guards his own palace, his goods are in peace. But when a stronger than he comes upon him and overcomes him, he takes from him all his armor in which he trusted, and divides his spoils."

First, notice Jesus' awesome power—He casts out demons with His finger! It's not a hard thing for Him to set you free from every oppressive imagination, thought, or stronghold. He's capable, powerful, and willing. Second, a demon is the strong man that sets up shop in your mind when a stronghold is established. He rules over that area and regards you as his unless someone stronger than he shows up to set the record straight.

That "someone," of course, is Jesus, who lives inside you and works through the power of the Holy Spirit. First John 4:4 KJV emphatically proclaims, "Greater is he that is in you, than he that is in the world." That means you've got the Greater One living inside you, and this Greater One is all you need to strip the devil of his power and take back all he has stolen from you.

Whatever attack you're facing—whether it's an imagination, high thought, or stronghold—doesn't have to control you and rule your life. The Greater One inside you is waiting for you to call upon His name and unleash His mighty power over every enemy tormenting you. Run to the cross, confess every sin, and call upon God's mercy and grace to deliver you. He will surely answer. Then, after you've experienced His wonderful delivering power, make up your mind to never go back into that bondage.

Allow the Holy Spirit to daily fill you and give you the strength and courage you need to resist every evil attack. When the devil comes knocking at your door again—and he surely will—you don't have to open it and invite him back in. Whatever the temptation, immediately reject it when it tries to come into your mind. Don't entertain it for an instant; it's too dangerous, and you're fooling yourself if you think you can control it.

Then verbally bind the devil, command him to leave you, and physically remove yourself from the temptation, if necessary. That means if you've been delivered from alcohol, don't stop by the bar on the way home from work. Don't even go down the liquor aisle in the grocery store. Cut off every opportunity to fall back into that sin. When the thought "One little drink wouldn't hurt" pops into your mind, immediately counter with "He whom the Son sets free is free indeed, and I am free because Jesus set me free." Then rebuke the enemy and begin praising God, worshiping Him for His grace extended to you right at that moment to keep you from falling.

I know this sounds simple, but living free of the devil is simple, if you'll do what the Word of God says to do. It doesn't matter what the particular temptation is—fear, depression, jealousy, anger, deception, adultery—*nothing* is more powerful than Jesus on the inside of you.

You are God's property, not the devil's. You belong to God alone when you come to the cross for salvation. God is your righteousness, healer, fortress, and banner. He's your shepherd, your provider, and the source of all peace. He was and is and is to come. He rules and reigns over all—and that includes every demon in hell!

Chapter 7

Let's Go to War!

Psalm 144, along with Psalm 18, has a great deal to say about spiritual warfare. Although the entire psalm is full of the imagery of war, I'd like to zero in on the last five verses in particular. In them I see four specific areas in which we need to go to war.

War for Your Family

In verse 11 of Psalm 144, David called upon the name of the Lord to rescue him from all his enemies. In verse 12 of the New International Version, he states the result of God's delivering power:

> Then our sons in their youth
> will be like well-nurtured plants,
> and our daughters will be like pillars
> carved to adorn a palace.

God wants to deliver you from every enemy. He wants no weapon formed against you to prosper, because He is full of good plans for you and your family. That plan, however, might not come to pass if you don't rise up and war on behalf of your family members.

No one else cares about your family as much as you do. That's only natural. Others may join you in prayer and be concerned with your family's problems, but no one else will jump into the thick of battle and war for your family with the same intensity of heart and spirit that you will. That is your responsibility, particularly for your children.

Like all parents, my wife and I have had to wage war against the enemy concerning many areas of our children's lives. I remember once when my second son, Jonathan, was five years old and plagued with numerous warts on his body. He had several on each hand and some on his side, elbow, and toes. I realize that warts are not really all that serious, but I don't want anything less than the absolute best for my children, so I didn't want those things on him. So Melanie and I began to pray and bind the devil from Jonathan's body.

Each night before bedtime, we took Jonathan's little hands into ours and commanded those warts to die. Jesus spoke to the fig tree and cursed it at the root, so we did the same thing, cursing those warts at the root and commanding them to die. We did this every night, faithfully and patiently.

Since Jonathan was only five, he didn't understand too much about what we were doing or why. He just knew that his mother and father were praying with him every night for those warts to disappear. We kept at it, but nothing seemed to change. Jonathan, in his childish innocence, asked, "Daddy, why are the warts still here? When are they going to go away?"

I didn't have a concrete answer for my little boy, but I knew the truth of God's Word, so I just encouraged him and said, "Sometimes it takes a little while. Those warts might not disappear in a moment, but if we keep praying, one of these days they *are* going to disappear." And Jonathan believed me.

Finally after many weeks, I was going through my usual bedtime routine with him when I noticed that one of his hands didn't have any warts. I quickly said, "Let me see your other hand." They were gone from that hand. I said, "Roll up your pajama sleeve." They were gone from his elbow. I said, "Pull up your shirt." They were gone from his side. I said, "Let me see your foot," and they were gone from there too. Every one of those pesky, lingering warts had disappeared. Jonathan had brand-new skin, just like he had never had any warts at all.

That's just one small example about how you can do warfare for your children. Your children are children of destiny, well-nurtured plants and pillars in the house of the Lord. They don't have to be juvenile delinquents bringing forth the devil's fruit. You can wage war on their behalf so that they will be a blessing to you, the church, and the world. But you're going to have to fight for them.

War for Your Finances

Psalm 144:13 NIV lists the next area in which you must wage personal warfare: your finances.

> Our barns will be filled
> with every kind of provision.
> Our sheep will increase by thousands,
> by tens of thousands in our fields.

God does want to bless you financially, but it does not happen automatically, with no resistance from the devil. Just like you do with your family, you are going to have to assume spiritual responsibility for the state of your finances. You and you alone are going to have to rise up and command the devil to relinquish his stranglehold over your money and possessions.

The devil wants you scrounging around for your daily bread so that you'll have no time, resources, or energy to invest in others or God's kingdom. It doesn't matter if you have a lot or a little—the devil will try to steal every bit of your financial resources. He attacks both the millionaire and the pauper; he is not partial. The fact that someone has great material wealth doesn't mean that he is immune to the devil's attacks, and the fact that someone is destitute doesn't mean the devil will leave him alone. Regardless of the amount you possess, the devil wants it!

When your financial resources are attacked, you win the victory the same way you win it concerning your children or in any other area. In effect, you will have to draw a line in the sand and say "No more!" to the devil. Then you'll have to use the authority that is yours as a child of God. There's nothing complicated about it and no "deeper" secret you have to learn. The tools are already at your disposal, but you have to decide if you will use them.

Let's suppose you don't have enough income to meet your monthly expenses. First, acknowledge that you have a shortage. That is not a "bad confession"; that's the truth of your current situation. Faith never requires you to deny reality but pushes you past the limits of reality. There's a difference, so acknowledge the problem while stating your confidence in God's willingness and ability to help. Begin to thank and praise Him for all He's done for you in the past and all He's going to do for you in your current situation. Continue in that vein for a while.

After you've spent some time professing your faith in God's Word and worshiping Him for His greatness, move into spiritual warfare. Boldly proclaim, "Devil, I bind you from stealing my financial provision. Greater is He who is in me than he who is in the world. In the name of the Lord, I command you to loose your hold from my finances and to get out of my life."

You might want to pick up your checkbook and use it as a point of contact in prayer. Believe God to show you ways to increase your financial wealth. Expect your bank account to grow and increase. Develop an expectant faith, and then go ahead and laugh at the devil. Yes, laugh! Let him know that you know the victory is certain. You've got nothing to fear, because you know that your God will surely answer.

War for Your Protection

The next area of personal warfare is found in verse 14 of Psalm 144:

That there be no breaking in or going out;
That there be no outcry in our streets.

This, I believe, refers to the area of protection. As a child of God, divine protection is yours. You have no need to fear that thieves and burglars are going to break into your home and steal everything you own. You have no need to fear that the high crime rate in your city means that you're the next victim. You don't have to worry that the airline you're flying on is going to be hijacked by terrorists. You have God's protection around you; read Psalm 91 if you don't believe it!

As I've stated before, being a Christian doesn't mean that nothing bad can ever happen to you, but it does mean that you don't have to live in fear of what might or might not happen to you. Those kinds of thoughts come from the devil. God, however, keeps whispering truth to you. "I'm watching your back," He says. "Nothing can touch you without going through Me first," He continues. "I'm in control of your life, not the devil," He affirms.

That's the proclamation of divine protection that you've got to throw back at the devil when he starts trying to make you afraid. When he throws a punch at you, you throw back an even harder one, knowing that the Holy One of Israel fights for you!

War for Your Happiness

Verse 15 of Psalm 144 sums up the results of what precedes it in verses 11–14:

Happy are the people who are in such a state;
Happy are the people whose God is the Lord!

When you go to war for your children, finances, and protection, you're going to be happy — not happy in the sense of always feeling good, but happy in the sense of having the joy of the Lord as a sustaining force in your life. When you rise up like a mighty warrior, there's a satisfaction that comes from assuming your rightful place in the army of God. Even if you think you are a coward at heart, something deep inside you wants to be a mighty man or woman of God. Even though you might feel like a mouse on the outside, you have the heart of a lion on the inside.

Exercising your spiritual clout against the enemy leads to spiritual victory, and this in turn causes your confidence in God to grow by leaps and bounds. As you see God moving in response to your prayers and actions, you find your faith growing. Your walk with God becomes exciting and challenging, and even when you face problems, you have enough maturity and experience to realize that what He did for you yesterday, He'll do again tomorrow and the next day. Joy becomes a way of life, not a fleeting emotion.

You are responsible for the degree to which you live in the joy of the Lord. You can just sit there every day and let the devil do whatever he wants, or you can pick up your sword and decapitate every demon from hell that comes against you. It's up to you. One choice leads to pain, suffering, and depression, while the other leads to endurance, victory, and joy.

Warring in the Heavenlies

As necessary as it is to war for your family, finances, protection, and happiness, there is an even more important reason why you need to learn spiritual warfare. God wants you to not only learn how to wage spiritual war on your own behalf, but he wants you to join Him in His plan of setting the captives free all around the world. God has not given you only the task of keeping yourself and your family free; He has also entrusted you with the responsibility of freeing the masses.

Until you are personally free and walking in freedom, you'll never be able to free anyone else. Although you do have to learn how to war for yourself, it should never stop there. Christianity is never about "What's in it for me?" It's always outward-focused, and that must be reflected in your spiritual warfare. There comes a time when you've got to move toward waging the war in the heavenlies against the powers that are enslaving millions around the world.

Do you realize that approximately one out of every five people in the world is Muslim? In India, the second most populous nation on earth, nearly 85 percent are followers of Hinduism. The countries of the world are filled with masses of teeming humanity who have no knowledge of the Savior and how He can set them free from bondage and false religion. They have no idea that freedom is even possible or that God sent His Son to liberate them from every evil plan of the enemy.

I once saw a documentary that really helped me understand this idea of liberation. Having been born after World War II, I had studied this great war in school but had never fully realized what took place in Europe during the Allied forces' final thrust. Beginning with the Normandy invasion in June of 1944, the Allied forces initiated a determined push inward to liberate all of Europe from Hitler's rule. The reason for this massive military thrust was clear: "to preserve . . . our civilization and to set free a suffering humanity," as President Franklin Roosevelt stated.

After the initial landing on the shores of Normandy, the Allied forces began the process of liberating France and then continued the push toward Germany. The enemy resisted mightily but was powerless against the combined Allied forces. Yard by yard, mile by mile, the Allied army liberated Europe one village at a time.

Accounts abound of the reactions of the people when the Allied forces rolled into their towns and they realized they had been set free from Hitler's tyranny. Flinging wide their windows, they celebrated wildly and with reckless abandon. They cried and shouted for joy and soon took to dancing and rejoicing in the streets with their liberators. Oh, the joy that exploded when those who had been held captive were suddenly set free!

The loss of life to liberate Europe was horrific, and the crosses of the fallen heroes still dot the Normandy countryside, but the purpose was clear: "to set free a suffering humanity." In a similar fashion, Jesus died on the cross to liberate humankind. Hebrews 2:14–15 tells why He did it: "that through death He might destroy him who had the power of death, that is, the devil, and release those who through fear of death were all their lifetime subject to bondage." All their lifetimes, people are subject to the devil's bondage until someone comes to liberate them. They cannot free themselves; they need God's army of mighty warriors who will proclaim the truth that Jesus came to set them free. I want to be part of that army, and I hope you do too.

The early church knew its purpose and lived it every day. When persecution arose in Jerusalem after Stephen's death, the disciples were dispersed throughout Judea and Samaria. One of the disciples, Philip, went to Samaria and began to preach Jesus' liberating power. "And the multitudes with one accord heeded the things spoken by Philip, hearing and seeing the miracles which he did. For unclean spirits, crying with a loud voice, came out of many who were possessed; and many who were paralyzed and lame were healed. And there was great joy in that city" (Acts 8:6–8). Philip knew how to set the captives free.

In Acts 19, we see Paul in Ephesus, a city that revered the goddess Diana. In the midst of this pagan culture, Paul went about the business of setting people free. "Now God worked unusual miracles by the hands of Paul, so that even handkerchiefs or aprons were brought from his body to the sick, and the diseases left them and the evil spirits went out of them" (vv. 11–12). The chapter continues, "Also, many of those who had practiced magic brought their books together and burned them in the sight of all. And they counted up the value of them, and it totaled fifty thousand pieces of silver. So the word of the Lord grew mightily and prevailed" (vv. 19–20).

Paul, Peter, Stephen, Barnabas, and all the other great men and women in Acts devoted their lives to setting the captives free. So single-minded was their focus and so successful were they in achieving their goal that they became known as "these who have turned the world upside down" (Acts 17:6). How'd you like someone to say that about you? How'd you like your faith to be so strong that your presence turned somebody's world upside down? That, my friend, is a warrior, and that is your calling in Christ.

Most of us Christians, unfortunately, never move into our destinies as bold, fearless warriors in the army of God. We seem to get stuck in first or second gear and never get quite enough power to make it into third. We're powerless against fear, depression, and lust. We feel like victims of our own weaknesses and dispositions. We swallow the devil's lies that it's good enough to just endure to the end and then slip into heaven. We have so little victory in our own lives that we don't see how we can possibly help anyone else.

It's time for the church to move past that—to put on the mighty armor of God and rise into the heavenlies to war against those demonic powers that are holding so many in bondage. The eternal destination of millions of souls hangs in the balance, and we must get busy with the Father's business of setting the captives free.

Wrestling with the Enemy

Ephesians 6:10–13 is probably the best-known and most often quoted Scripture passage regarding spiritual warfare. Verse 10 starts the passage with these words: "Finally, my brethren, be strong in the Lord and in the power of His might." Now it doesn't say be strong *for* the Lord; it says be strong *in* the Lord. If you try to be strong *for* the Lord, you're destined to fail because you have no power within you. Willpower will take you only so far—and not very far at that! On the other hand, if you are strong *in* the Lord, then you look to Him as the source of your power. That means that all His resources are at your disposal, including His armor.

Verse 11 makes it quite apparent that this armor belongs to God, not us: "Put on the whole armor of God, that you may be able to stand against the wiles of the devil." Only God's armor will empower you to stand against the devil's tricks. Your strategies, plans, and ideas are useless against him. You have to fight the devil God's way, and the first thing to do is to put on God's armor so that you can be protected in the battle.

Verse 12 gives a really precise image of the kind of battle we're fighting: "For we do not wrestle against flesh and blood, but against principalities, against powers, against the rulers of the darkness of this age, against spiritual hosts of wickedness in the heavenly places." The word *wrestle* in this verse calls to mind a sport that is indicative of spiritual warfare. If you can get a clearer picture of what happens in the sport of wrestling, you'll also gain a clearer picture of what happens in spiritual warfare.

Merriam-Webster's Collegiate Dictionary, Eleventh Edition describes the verb *wrestle* in this way: "to contend by grappling with and striving to trip or throw an opponent down or off balance." The dictionary definition says that a wrestler attempts to catch his opponent off guard so that he can trip him up or throw him down. Thus wrestling is a sport of training, quickness, and agility rather than a sport of brute strength.

The sport of wrestling is not just two men bear-hugging and trying to push each other down. Unlike wrestling for entertainment, the sport of wrestling is quite serious and adheres to an exacting code of conduct and rules. During the course of the match, the two opponents may not seem to be doing much of anything at first. They may give the appearance of being locked in a stalemate, but really they are testing the agility of the other, pushing a little here and a little there to find a weakness they can exploit.

This is exactly what happens in spiritual warfare. When you lock up with the devil in a spiritual wrestling match, he doesn't just step out of the way and give in to your initial, tentative resistance. He will readily engage you and start testing your spiritual agility. He gives a push here and a nudge there, just to test your resolve. He continues to circle, looking for your point of vulnerability. He's in no hurry; he waits for the opportune moment to trip you up so he can pin you to the ground.

Wrestling is unlike other sports in that the game can be over in a split second if one of the players gets pinned by his opponent. Thus wrestlers must constantly be on the defensive, watching carefully lest they give their opponents even a slight advantage that can take them down. They must be perpetually diligent because one false move and they will find themselves lying flat on their backs under their opponents.

This is why Paul says in Ephesians 6:13, "Therefore take up the whole armor of God, that you may be able to withstand in the evil day, and having done all, to stand." When you're warring against the devil, above all you must stand! You've got to stay on your feet, and you can never, never lie down and play dead against him. You can't fool him; he'll only go in for the kill if he sees you lying down. As long as you're standing, however, you're still in the fight.

When you're standing against the enemy, time is irrelevant. Don't be concerned with how long the battle is taking or how nothing seems to be changing. Stay on guard, and stay on your feet. Eventually you'll be the one to throw the devil flat on his back and pin him to the ground.

Some of you have been standing a long time, and you're growing tired in the battle. You've been waiting for that wayward child to return home. You've been waiting for your finances to turn around. You've been waiting for a healing to manifest in your body. That's okay; just *keep standing!*

With one slight change in strategy, the entire course of a wrestling match can quickly change. Just about the time it looks like one man is ready to pin the other, his opponent, in the blink of an eye, thinks of a brilliant counterattack and instead pins him. In a split second, everything reverses, and the one who was on the bottom is now on top.

When you're waging war against the devil, about the time you think you're making no progress and actually think you're about to go down, the Holy Spirit will whisper a last-minute strategy in your ear. When you obey that prompting, all of a sudden everything changes. It doesn't matter how long you've been standing and how hopeless the situation seems; everything reverses in a split second.

Engaging the enemy really is so similar to a wrestling match. Remember that, and you'll come out on top every time!

Understanding the Lineup

In team sports, such as football, teams assign players to certain specific positions with corresponding duties. This is what we mean when we talk about a particular team's lineup. Before any game, a team is usually quite interested in its opponent's lineup. It wants to know who is filling which position and what that player's weaknesses and strengths are. This gives the team members advance preparation for what they might face in the game.

Athletes are meticulous in getting to know their opponents. They diligently study films of their opponents in action, scrutinizing every person in the lineup and memorizing every player's pattern of behavior. They get so familiar with the members of the opposing team that they can practically predict what they are going to do in any given situation. By the time the confrontation rolls around, they have a pretty good idea of what to expect from the opposing team.

Unlike athletes, Christians are by and large totally ignorant of their spiritual opponent. They don't study about Satan and learn his tactics. They don't recognize his maneuvers and certainly don't know how to fight him. Is it any wonder that so much of the church is weak, powerless, and impotent?

The cure for the problem is to study the opposing team's lineup and become familiar with its ways. The twelfth verse of Ephesians 6 lists several specific types of players on Satan's team (principalities, powers, rulers of darkness, hosts of wickedness). Much has been written about and preached concerning these levels, but let's take a brief look at each.

Principalities

The first and highest level of demonic resistance is principalities. Principalities are executive rulers of darkness, the "idea people" of the devil's kingdom. We could compare them to the executive branch of the government. In other words, they are the ones in charge and at the top in the chain of command.

Principalities align themselves with geopolitical boundaries or with nations. We find this example in the book of Daniel. In an angelic visitation, Daniel was told the following: "Do not fear, Daniel, for from the first day that you set your heart to understand, and to humble yourself before your God, your words were heard; and I have come because of your words. But the *prince of the kingdom of Persia* withstood me twenty-one days; and behold, Michael, one of the chief princes, came to help me, for I had been left alone there with the kings of Persia" (Dan. 10:12–13, emphasis added).

The angel was opposed by a demonic entity in control of the specific geographic region known as Persia (modern-day Iran). For twenty-one days, the battle raged between the kingdom of darkness and the kingdom of light, until Michael, a prince in God's kingdom, lent his support to defeat the demonic principality.

I personally believe that Satan assigns principalities over the nations of the world, and I believe this level of demonic influence consists of those who, like Satan, were formerly high-level beings in God's kingdom before their rebellion. When Satan fell from heaven, they fell with him, and he has given them authority over high levels in his kingdom.

Principalities cause darkness to prevail over entire nations or regions. I once heard a missionary story about two nations whose boundary lay right down the middle of a particular street. On one side of the street, the missionaries could pass out tracts and the people would eagerly take them and read them, but on the other side of the street, no one was even interested. The demonic principality over one nation was obviously more powerful than in the other and exerted its evil influence over the hearts and minds of the people there.

Powers and Rulers of Darkness

The next two levels of demonic influence are called powers and rulers of darkness. These spirits execute the orders issued by the principalities. They are dominating spirits that rule over an area in order to accomplish the goals of the higher spiritual principality that is in charge. In other words, the principalities stake out claim to national or geographic areas, and the powers and rulers concentrate on specific areas of wickedness in those nations.

The principality has a game plan for the region—to steal, kill, and destroy—and the powers more specifically carry out the plan. For example, there may be prevailing spirits of murder, sexual immorality, or poverty over certain regions; these are specific spirits at work to carry out the destructive strategy of the principality in charge.

Hosts of Wickedness

At this lower level, we find the specific, individual demons at work, the foot soldiers, so to speak, in Satan's army. These are the fiends who whisper all kinds of evil into the ears of anyone who will listen. They're the ones who entice you to sin, telling you you're not hurting anyone. They work in any and all areas, but they work in conjunction with the powers, rulers of darkness, and principalities to see God's kingdom and people destroyed or at least weakened to the point of ineffectiveness. This is the level of spiritual resistance that you will probably deal most extensively with in your day-to-day life.

Four Areas of Warfare

In the remainder of this chapter, I have selected four specific areas that I see as the greatest threats to our nation. I realize other people might identify different ones, but these are the four that I think have a particularly strong grip on our land. These are the areas that I target in intercessory prayer for our nation.

Spirit of Murder

Few would deny the prevalence of violence and murder in our society. Movies, television, and popular music are full of the most horrific images of death and destruction, all presented in the form of "entertainment" and defended as "freedom of expression." It seems as though murder is rampant, and the ways of the murderer becoming more vile, more cruel, and more unimaginable by the day.

All kinds of reasons could be given as to why our society is so violent, but at the deepest level, I believe, is a demonic spirit at work. This spirit has been in operation for centuries in many lands, and we are seeing its evil face in our country. How else do you explain a nation that will turn its back and look the other way while millions of its children are sacrificed to the spirit of abortion? America has done exactly that in the thirty-three years since *Roe v. Wade* took precedence.

As horrible as abortion is, killing children is not a new thing, because the spirit that inspires it is not a new thing. It's been around for many, many years, as evidenced in the Bible. In several places, the Old Testament talks about Chemosh and Molech, gods of the Moabites and Ammonites, to whom infants were offered. Parents actually took their precious babies and laid them in the arms of these false gods and burned them alive. Nothing but a horribly wicked spirit could entice a person to do that.

I once had a vision in which I saw this spirit of murder lurking underground in a particular nation. I saw people in this land feeding babies to a god, and I asked God for the meaning of what I was seeing. One word, *Chemosh*, came to me. I was not familiar with that word at the time, but when I looked it up, I discovered this name in the Bible. I saw then that there is a specific demon spirit that likes to destroy human beings.

Why would a demon want to murder innocent, defenseless babies? The answer is found in Psalm 8:2: "From the lips of children and infants you have ordained praise" (NIV). Children and babies seem to have an innate ability to worship. There is nothing more pure and precious than watching these little ones clap their tiny hands and raise their chubby arms to Jesus. They love Him so innocently, and the devil can't stand that. He absolutely hates their pure, untainted praise, so he seeks to destroy them. He is totally evil and totally ruthless in his plan to get rid of as many children as he can.

Spirit of Immorality

The second prevailing spirit that I see at work in our nation is a spirit of sexual immorality and perversion. Never before have premarital sex and homosexuality been so openly flaunted as they are today. Some parents and schools assume their teens will inevitably have sex and think the best they can do is to teach them how to have "safe sex." They think it's too old-fashioned to actually expect anyone to wait until marriage before engaging in sex.

That's bad enough, but perhaps even more disturbing is the homosexual agenda that seeks not only to gain tolerance for an aberrant lifestyle, but also to proclaim it as a wonderful, viable alternative to heterosexuality. Don't be deceived; there is no alternative to God's Word and the functions He relegated to male and female. Homosexuality is not normal behavior, and it is not accepted by God as an alternative lifestyle.

I truly feel for the homosexual caught in this lie. As long as he is in the grip of that spirit, he is blind to his true condition. He has the media and the world around him telling him how brave he is to come out of the closet, but he doesn't see the darkness he's walking into. He's deceived, victim to the lies of the father of lies.

This spirit of sexual immorality is so dangerous because it appeals to human passions and pleasures. People have an extraordinary ability to believe whatever benefits them, so when someone comes along who says "If it feels good, do it!" they are more than ready to listen to him.

That's why we need the Word of God. It sets standards and boundaries that God Himself has drawn. It affords a protection that we cannot give ourselves. It contains all truth and wisdom, irrespective of the opinions of man. That's to be our standard—not what the world proclaims as "new" and "enlightened." Isaiah 5:20 makes this clear:

> Woe to those who call evil good, and good evil;
> Who put darkness for light, and light for darkness;
> Who put bitter for sweet, and sweet for bitter!

Their end is deception and destruction.

Sexual immorality—and homosexuality in particular—is so offensive because it mocks the image of God in man. The Bible clearly states that sexual relations are reserved for a man and a woman in the context of marriage. When demons entice unmarried people to partake of something reserved for married couples, they mock the institution of marriage. When they persuade men to have sex with men and women with women, they mock the God-created differences and complementary functions of the male and female bodies. It is a perversion of what God made sex to be, and demons always want to pervert the truth. It's part of their nature as deceivers.

Spirit of Humanism

A third spirit we need to recognize is the spirit of humanism. This basically is a spirit that exalts man over God. Humanism, in effect, worships man, because humanists believe in man's ability for self-realization through the use of reason.

The mind is indeed a wonderful thing, and God does want us to use our intellects, but anytime human knowledge is exalted as the standard of enlightened knowledge, something's wrong. Human knowledge is finite, but God's is infinite. God alone is the source of all wisdom, so if any of us have even a smidgeon of knowledge, we got it from God.

Humanists don't see it this way. They extol the advancement of the human race and how much we have achieved over the ages. They think humankind is capable of solving any problem if we will all just work together and reason out the answers. They like to paint a rosy-colored picture of the wonderful world humans are going to create, but it's an illusion. Human beings will never be able to solve the world's problems because they are not God. Reason and wisdom are limited. Only an acknowledgment of God's supremacy over humankind can turn the tide in the downward spiral of humanity.

Humanists pretty much allow anything in the name of human rights. If you want to have an abortion, that's okay. It's your "right." Want to have a homosexual lover? That's okay, too; in fact, the humanist will laud you for your enlightened views and champion you for your bold courage. And what about the content of television, movies, and other forms of art? According to the humanist, anything goes because you have a "right" to express yourself in any way you choose, even if others find it vile, offensive, or sacrilegious.

Spirit of Religion

It may surprise you to see religion listed as a spirit, but it can be when it takes the place of true worship of God. This religious spirit is actually a form of witchcraft because it replaces worship and service to God with manmade laws, traditions, and rituals. A religious spirit is particularly dangerous because it has a form of godliness but denies its power (2 Tim. 3:5).

People with a religious spirit often think they are very spiritual. They may devote hours to doing all kinds of things that make them feel good about themselves. However, the emphasis is on self and good works, not on the power of the blood of Jesus to save.

The devil loves for you to think you're religious, because if you stay busy doing all kinds of things to prove your love for God and other people, you won't recognize your own desperate need for God. You might go to church every Sunday and on Wednesday nights too. Maybe you sing in the choir, and maybe you tithe 10 percent to the church. You might volunteer to be on every committee and never say no to any project you're asked to help with. As good as all these things are, they cannot take the place of a personal relationship with Jesus Christ as Lord and Savior. Unless these actions are a reflection of an existing relationship with Christ, they count for nothing.

Religion keeps you jumping through all kinds of hoops and so busy with "spiritual" activity that you have no time to just enjoy God and other people. Once you get on the religious treadmill, there's no getting off, because no matter how much you do, it is never enough. You can never satisfy a religious spirit; it always requires more. Unless you deal with it, you'll go right on being religious and end up going to hell—good deeds and all!

The world is not going to get better and better. It will only continue to get worse and worse until Christ returns.

If ever there was a time for the church to rise up and war in the heavenlies, it's now. Principalities, powers, rulers of darkness, and hosts of wickedness are ours, if we'll rise up against them. Spirits of murder, immorality, humanism, and religion can be abolished, if we'll go to battle. If we'll march in the knowledge of Christ and His glorious power within us, we'll be a mighty invincible army capable of taking on any demon from hell. It's time for us to rise up. It's time for us to war!

Chapter 8

The Liberators

We are called to be liberators, to set the captives free and loose the bonds of wickedness holding them prisoners. Our calling is high and sure to be victorious because we war in the strength of the Greater One living inside of us. Most of us, unfortunately, really don't grasp the extent of that mighty power residing within. We sell ourselves short and actually cower and shrink from any confrontation with the enemy.

If we ever get the revelation of how powerful we really are, there will be no stopping the advance of God's kingdom. The devil knows that and thus tries his hardest to keep us ignorant of the fact. But in this last chapter, I want to show you the truth of what you can do when you release the mighty power of God and step into your role as a warrior in God's army.

Look at what 2 Samuel 22:38–41 says:

I have pursued my enemies and destroyed them;
Neither did I turn back again till they were destroyed.
And I have destroyed them and wounded them,
So that they could not rise;
They have fallen under my feet.
For You have armed me with strength for the battle;

You have subdued under me those who rose against me.
You have also given me the necks of my enemies,
So that I destroyed those who hated me.

I like that, don't you? Bold, powerful, impassioned words from a conquering warrior-king. David was not afraid of his enemies; he pursued them until he caught them, and then he destroyed them. He totally annihilated them so that they could never trouble him again.

I especially like the imagery at the end of the passage: "You have also given me the necks of my enemies." In David's day, when a king conquered another king, he made a very visible demonstration of his victory. The subdued king was forced to prostrate himself before the conquering king. As he lay there with his nose in the dirt, the victorious king would put his foot on the neck of his vanquished foe, publicly demonstrating his superior power. It was a glorious day for the triumphant king.

Christians spend so much of their time talking about the devil—how big, bad, and ugly he is—and running scared from him. They just don't know the power they have. If they did, they would whirl around, knock the devil flat, and pin his neck to the ground! They'd do like David did:

Then I beat them as fine as the dust of the earth;
I trod them like dirt in the streets,
And I spread them out (v. 43).

That's what a victor does.

Jesus, of course, was fully confident in His power. When He walked the earth, His very presence tormented demon powers. Even when He did not address them, they recognized His power and cowered before Him. The demons in the demoniac from Gadara begged Jesus not to torment them and not to cast them into the abyss (Luke 8:28, 31). They knew that they were completely powerless before Jesus and that He had total authority over them.

If you have Jesus living inside of you, then you have access to that same kind of power. Because you are confident in who Jesus is, you can be confident of what He will do through you. You were never meant to live in fear and trembling before any person or demon power. You were meant to be every bit a conquering king, with your foot on your enemy's neck and a shout of victory in your mouth.

David's Mighty Men

Verses 8–11 of 2 Samuel 23 spotlight David's three mightiest men: Adino (also known as Josheb-Basshebeth the Tachmonite), Eleazar, and Shammah. David had many mighty men, but these three guys were distinguished among all the rest. They were incredible warriors because David had communicated and demonstrated to them how to do warfare. They had not only observed his example but had also imitated it, and in the course of events, they became mighty in their own right. When David became king, these mighty men of valor became his most trusted advisors and aides. Let's look at these men and the qualities they exhibited.

David's Three Mightiest

Adino was "chief of the Three; he raised his spear against eight hundred men, whom he killed in one encounter" (v. 8 NIV). The Bible doesn't relate how this happened, only that it did, but obviously Adino had supernatural strength and ability that enabled him to do something unheard of and unmatched by anyone else. Adino was no pansy; he was full of power, vigor, and brute force. I can just imagine how intimidating he must have been. Only a completely confident, self-assured man would even dare to lift his spear against so many, much less expect to be victorious. But that's the kind of warrior

Adino was, and that's what made him chief among David's top three warriors.

Verses 9 and 10 tell us about Eleazar, another of David's three mightiest men. "As one of the three mighty men, he was with David when they taunted the Philistines gathered at Pas Dammim for battle. Then the men of Israel retreated, but he stood his ground and struck down the Philistines till his hand grew tired and froze to the sword" (NIV).

We don't know how many men Eleazar slew, but he fought so long and hard that his hand was glued to the hilt of his sword. He had determination, grit, and perseverance like no one else. The Scriptures say that "he stood his ground." Everybody else ran from the Philistines like a scared rabbit, but when the battle was over, Eleazar remained standing. All the soldiers who had fled crept back and helped him pick up the spoils of battle (v. 10).

The third mighty man was Shammah, and he proved his mettle when the Philistines attacked the Israelites in a field of lentils. Everyone else fled, but Shammah "stationed himself in the middle of the field, defended it, and killed the Philistines" (v. 12). Once again a fierce battle raged, and defeat looked imminent. Just when everyone else had given up and run for their lives, one man, Shammah, stood up and said, "I'll not retreat; I'll not run from the enemy. The rest of you can do what you want, but as for me, I'll not back down!"

Shammah's name actually means "The Lord is here," or "The Lord is with me," and his name is indicative of his actions. He knew that if God was on his side, then it didn't matter how many were against him. He knew that he and God made a majority against any force on earth. He knew that when everyone else forsakes you, God is still there. That was the source of his strength and courage, and it gave him a tenacity that no one else could understand.

These three men were awesome, and their valor and boldness did not diminish. The passage of time only made them more daring. Their confidence grew, and their loyalty to David, their example and king, was unbelievable. Once when David was in the cave of Adullam, he expressed a desire for a drink of water from a specific well in Bethlehem. At that time, the Philistines occupied Bethlehem, so David could not just stroll into the city and get a drink of water. It was impossible because an enemy controlled the town.

David did not actually ask his men to get him a drink; he only expressed a longing. But the three mighty men so loved their commander that they decided to slip away and get him water from the well in Bethlehem (2 Sam. 23:13–16). They were determined that their master would get whatever he desired, even if it entailed great physical risk to themselves.

There's a lesson to be learned from these three mighty men. Even if you are a bold, courageous warrior in your own right, your ability to wage war is not meant to be used only for you and your wishes. God has made you a warrior so that you can go to the front and jump into the battle for any cause that He desires. His wish must become your command, and your desire must be to fulfill your Lord's every longing.

God did not save you just for you to be happy, protected, prosperous, and blessed. He saved you and called you to be a liberator. God's deepest desire is not just that you be kept from the evil one, but that you learn how to destroy the devil on his own territory. You're called to set the captives free.

David's Thirty

In addition to the Three, David had another group of thirty valiant men known for their courage and daring. The rest of chapter 23 lists them and some of their exploits. In particular, Benaiah, the son of Jehoiada, stands out. This dauntless warrior killed two of Moab's mightiest warriors, chased a lion into a pit on a snowy day and killed it, and fearlessly disarmed an Egyptian and slew him. There seemed to be no limit to this man's courage.

In speaking of the Egyptian, verse 21 in this chapter says, "And he killed an Egyptian, a spectacular man. The Egyptian had a spear in his hand; so he went down to him with a staff, wrested the spear out of the Egyptian's hand, and killed him with his own spear." Notice that the Egyptian was described as "spectacular." In other words, he was a fearsome, huge, awesome man, not some lily-livered flunky that anybody could take on. But Benaiah was not fazed by the man's size or the fact that the Egyptian was better armed. He just marched right up to that big man, plucked the spear from his hand, and killed him with it!

How did he do it? I don't know, but something on the inside of Benaiah knew that he was invincible, and that was conveyed to his enemy. When the Lord is mobilized with you and you know it, you can walk right up to any demon power, grab the spear from his hand, and pin him to the wall with it. That's how fearless you are when you know the Holy One of Israel is living on the inside of you.

Liberating the Nations

God raises up liberators to liberate entire nations. We see this in Isaiah 45, when Isaiah, two hundred years before the birth of King Cyrus, prophesied of God's intention to use Cyrus for His divine purposes. Tradition says that one of the reasons that Cyrus allowed the Jews to return to Jerusalem was the fact that they showed him his own name in the Scriptures. That so convinced him of the superiority of the God of Israel that he allowed them to return to their home.

Look at what the Bible foretold two hundred years before it came to pass:

> This is what the Lord says to Cyrus, his anointed one, whose right hand he will empower. Before him, mighty kings will be paralyzed with fear. Their fortress gates will

be opened, never again to shut against him. This is what the Lord says: "I will go before you, Cyrus, and level the mountains. I will smash down gates of bronze and cut through bars of iron. And I will give you treasures hidden in the darkness—secret riches. I will do this so you may know that I am the Lord, the God of Israel, the one who calls you by name" (Isa. 45:1–3 NLT).

In other words, God said, "Cyrus, I'm going to put fear in your enemies. They'll not be able to stand against you. I'm going to destroy every barrier in your path, and then I'm going to give you the treasures that your enemy has been hiding from you."

Brothers and sisters, this is what warfare does. It removes the enemy's power over individuals, cities, and nations. It looses the greatest treasure in the world—human souls—from the grip of the devil and makes it possible to bring them the Gospel. God sovereignly planned and used a king who didn't even know Him in order to accomplish His purposes; how much more can He use those of us who are surrendered to Him and His will?

From the very beginning, God knows the plans He has for individuals. We've already seen part of His plan for Cyrus, and in Jeremiah 1:5, we see His awesome plan for Jeremiah the prophet:

"Before I formed you in the womb I knew you;
Before you were born I sanctified you;
I ordained you a prophet to the nations."

Verses 9 and 10 continue,

"Behold, I have put My words in your mouth.
See, I have this day set you over the nations and over the kingdoms,

To root out and to pull down,
To destroy and to throw down,
To build and to plant."

Then in chapter 51, verse 20, God says,

"You are My battle-ax and weapons of war:
For with you I will break the nation in pieces;
With you I will destroy kingdoms."

How awesome to think that God made plans for you even before you were born! Part of that plan is for you to be a mighty warrior, speaking His words and pulling down every kingdom that is against His. He's called you to be a weapon in His hand—to be His battle-ax!

When we hear the word *battle-ax,* most of us think of a sharp-tongued, domineering woman, perhaps a strict school-teacher. We've come to associate it with that image of a mean, humorless woman that we dare not cross—even if our lives depended upon it. That is one use of the word, but a battle-ax is also an actual weapon of war used in times past. It had two sharp edges and was sometimes mounted on a long stick to give the one using it greater scope and leverage. When a soldier started swinging that weapon of war, hair, teeth, and eyeballs went flying! No one could stand before it, so powerful was it.

In God's eyes, you are a mighty battle-ax, a weapon of war to strike terror in the heart of the enemy. When God starts swinging you around, demons are going to bail out in every direction. The kingdom of darkness is going to topple, and you are going to affect nations when you yield yourself as a weapon of war in God's hands.

Like Jeremiah and Cyrus, Daniel, too, was a liberator, and God used him to set a nation free. Daniel's primary weapon was prayer, and so mighty an intercessor was he that God could entrust him with powerful visions and super-natural insight. We've already read in Daniel 10:12 how his prayers brought breakthrough in the spiritual realm against demonic principalities. Even though he saw no change in the outward, he continued praying and standing until the angels broke through with a message from the Lord. As a result, the entire course of the Jewish nation was altered.

Jesus, the Great Liberator

As great as the liberation was that came from Cyrus, Jeremiah, and Daniel, Jesus brought an even greater kind of liberation. He, of course, could do what they as men could never do. They could offer only political liberation, but Jesus came to bring spiritual liberation from the kingdom of darkness. He proclaimed this in Luke 4:18:

> "The Spirit of the Lord is upon Me,
> Because He has anointed Me
> To preach the gospel to the poor;
> He has sent Me to heal the brokenhearted,
> To proclaim liberty to the captives
> And recovery of sight to the blind,
> To set at liberty those who are oppressed;
> To proclaim the acceptable year of the Lord."

In other words, Jesus was saying, "My whole mission is to set people free, to give them the Good News that there is healing, liberty, and wholeness in Me, to let them know that the Year of Jubilee has come."

Immediately following this proclamation, Jesus went about the business of setting the captives free. He went to the synagogue in Capernaum and encountered "a man who had a spirit of an unclean demon. And he cried out with a loud voice, saying, 'Let us alone! What have we to do with

You, Jesus of Nazareth? Did You come to destroy us? I know who You are—the Holy One of God!' " (Luke 4:33–34). The devil's first line of defense was to try to persuade Jesus to just leave him alone. Although Jesus had just declared His mission and calling to set the captives free, the devil still tried to dissuade Him from it.

Jesus, of course, could not be deterred from loosing the man held captive. He refused to negotiate, discuss, or make any deals with the devil. Ignoring the devil's tactics, He immediately went about the business of liberation. Jesus took authority over the demon in the man, ordered it to be quiet, and then cast it out quickly (v. 35).

Jesus didn't entertain demons or give them a platform from which to speak. He refused to be distracted from His sole purpose of setting the captives free. He was single-minded and sure of His ability to perform the task at hand.

I know some people get all excited about talking to demons, but that's not what Jesus did. He let them know who was boss, and that's what you should do too. The devil would love to engage you in irrelevant conversation all night long until you get so tired of talking that you just give up and leave him alone. But follow Jesus' pattern and say, "Be quiet and come out!" That's all it takes when a liberator comes on the scene.

One of the most beautiful things in the world to witness is the deliverance of someone that the devil has been holding in bondage. The process itself might get rather ugly, but when the demon leaves, the peace of God absolutely radiates from that person's face. Joy floods his being, and many times sanity and physical wholeness are restored.

Deliverance brings much glory to God because the change in the person is so obvious. When the demon came out of the man in the synagogue, the people "were all amazed and spoke among themselves, saying, 'What a word this is! For with authority and power He commands the unclean spirits, and they come out' " (v. 36). Notice they marveled at His word—not at His discussions or arguments with the unclean spirit. Jesus, full of authority, simply commanded the unclean spirit in the man to come out, and it had no choice but to obey.

Your Authority As a Liberator

One of the most marvelous gifts God gives us is authority in Christ. Jesus told us, "Most assuredly, I say to you, he who believes in Me, the works that I do he will do also; and greater works than these he will do, because I go to My Father" (John 14:12). That means you have the right and ability to cast out demons when they make their presence known. You really do have that power, because you have Christ living inside of you.

The devil, of course, will try to keep that truth from you. If you even dare think it, he'll boast, "You can't cast me out. I'm going to eat your lunch if you even try!" And some of you immediately back down and say, "Okay, maybe you're right. I'll just mind my own business." You need to understand, however, that he's simply calling your bluff to see if you know who you are in Christ. He's trying to stop you before you ever get started.

If you make it past that obstacle, he'll try another tactic. "I know all that you've done," he'll whisper. "You're such a sinner; God would never use someone like you." Many Christians let this demon of guilt and condemnation stop them. But you've got to rise up and declare, "No, devil, the blood of Jesus cleanses me from all sin. I'm covered in His blood; now come out!"

Then he'll start whining and pleading. He'll say all kinds of crazy, irrelevant things just to distract you. I've even encountered people who seem to fall asleep when you start trying to cast the devil out of them. I actually experienced that once.

In that encounter, a man approached me and said, "I would like to receive the baptism in the Holy Spirit."

"Fine, brother," I enthusiastically answered. "Have you made Jesus your Savior and forgiven everyone who has sinned against you?" I asked.

The man started to reply to my question, but at that point, a demon began to manifest. The man started yawning as I talked to him. Then he began to nod off, just falling asleep while I tried to talk to him. We were having a normal conversation one minute, and then the next minute this distinguished, dignified-looking man began nodding off.

At first I thought, "Well that's a strange way to receive the Holy Spirit." I really didn't realize what was going on, but then the Spirit of God revealed to me that it was a demon spirit, not the Holy Spirit, causing the man to act so strangely.

Immediately I got some other men to join me in binding that demon. As we prayed, the man began shaking and trembling, but we ignored his reaction and continued warring for about another minute. Then, all of a sudden, the man fell to the ground. He soon sat up, however, and the joy of God shone from his face as he began speaking in tongues. Just like that! That man was totally transformed by his encounter with God's power to deliver, and he hit the ground running. That's what happens when you step into the role of liberator.

In Luke 10:19, Jesus said, "Behold, I give you the authority to trample on serpents and scorpions, and over all the power of the enemy, and nothing shall by any means hurt you." That was His mandate to His disciples, and that is the authority He gave you too. Nothing—absolutely nothing—has power over you. You were meant to wear the victor's crown, to totally subjugate all demon powers that come against you. You were created to be a liberator.

In verse 21 of Luke 10, we see Jesus' reaction to His disciples' taking their first steps as liberators. After they returned to Him and told Him that even demons were subject to them in His name, "Jesus rejoiced in the Spirit and said, 'I thank You, Father, Lord of heaven and earth, that You have hidden these things from the wise and prudent and revealed them to babes. Even so, Father, for so it seemed good in Your sight.' "

Jesus rejoiced to see His disciples stepping into their positions of authority. That reveals a very poignant picture of how Jesus feels when you finally begin walking in the authority He has given you. He *rejoices,* much like a proud parent of a child who's learned a new skill. He's proud of you when you dare to believe His word that you are a powerful liberator.

It takes a childlike, trusting heart to believe what Jesus says, to acknowledge that there are such things as demons. Too many Christians, however, refuse to believe the simple truth of Scripture that demons exist because it sounds too far out or medieval. They never step into their role as liberators. But the Father reveals His truth to the children of faith, and these children use the authority of their Father to set the captives free.

The Violent Take It by Force

In Matthew 11:12, Jesus said, "From the days of John the Baptist until now the kingdom of heaven suffers violence, and the violent take it by force." We often think of Jesus as meek and mild, and He was, in the sense of being surrendered to the Father. However, there is another side to Jesus that we sometimes overlook. Jesus is the Lion of the tribe of Judah, and in that role, He is ruthless against every demonic power. He knows that there is a time for violent warring, and He knows the force it takes to accomplish God's will.

John the Baptist was the last prophet under the old dispensation. During that time, there was little casting out of devils and spiritual warfare. When Jesus stepped onto the stage of world history, however, all that changed. Now liberation was possible, but it was not going to automatically happen. Demons would continue to violently wage war to keep people in bondage, and God's people were going to have to learn how to violently resist them in order to appropriate kingdom blessings.

In the context of Matthew 11:12, the word *violent* refers to the action of seizing or snatching something. It's not a polite exchange of words, but a forceful taking. What is the devil holding back from you? Don't beg him for it—snatch it from him! That's what it means when it says "The violent take it by force."

One point I want to emphasize is that the violence I am referring to is spiritual. Physical violence is never God's way; it is the devil's way. You can never justify physical violence against a person, institution, or organization by using this verse from Matthew. That means you don't bomb abortion clinics or take the law into your hands. You bombard the heavens and wage spiritual war—violently—until you see the situation change.

The devil will torment you as long as you permit it. Until you rise up and violently rebuke him, he'll hang around and keep digging his claws into you. The late John Osteen once told a story that I think illustrates this perfectly. Brother Osteen said that he once had a vision in which a minister in a room was surrounded by demons. Brother Osteen saw one demon sitting on a throne and other large beings present also. These demons began wrapping up and binding the minister; then they took him off to another place.

As Brother Osteen watched, he realized that the demons intended to make him their next victim. Something rose up on the inside of him, however, and he marched up to the demon sitting on the throne and said, "You're not going to bring me into bondage, in Jesus' name." With those words, he turned around and walked out of the room. With that, the vision ended.

About a month later, Brother Osteen suddenly developed an irrational fear of flying. Flying had never bothered him before, but now the thought of it terrified him. Like a dark cloud, that bondage descended upon him for about a year. He canceled all speaking engagements that required him to fly but kept preaching at his church. As the year went by, he became more and more defeated and dejected as he walked in the grip of this bondage.

Then one day the Lord reminded him of the vision he had had. Brother Osteen realized that he had gone into bondage, just like the minister in his vision. The Lord then prompted, "Don't you remember what you did in the dream?"

Faith arose in Brother Osteen's heart, and he violently took a stand against the devil. He proclaimed the Word of God and announced, "Devil, I'll take my liberty—right now—from the fear of airplanes!" He turned around, walked out of the room, and made a reservation on a flight to another city in Texas. He didn't need to go there; he just needed to make his stand against the devil. His wife took him to the airport, he boarded the plane, he flew to the other city, he disembarked, he got on another plane, and he flew back home. He was free!

You have to get pushy with the devil. You have to get right up in his face and look at him eyeball to eyeball. You have to plant your feet, hold your stance, and never, never back up. Keep exerting that force until he crumbles—and he will—as you violently, forcefully press in.

Ushering in God's Kingdom

In Matthew 12:28, Jesus said, "If I cast out demons by the Spirit of God, surely the kingdom of God has come upon you." When you cast out devils, you are ushering in God's kingdom and in a very visible way proclaiming His greatness. The Spirit of God within you is greater than any evil spirit, and He is your greatest ally in spiritual warfare. His power working from within you is what makes you a liberator capable of establishing God's kingdom on earth.

When you step into the role of liberator, you have several tools at your disposal to help you win every spiritual battle. When you learn how to use these weapons, your spiritual warfare becomes targeted, effective, and powerful. With them, you can become a courageous warrior ushering in God's kingdom on the earth. Let's look at several of these tools.

Praying in the Spirit

In Ephesians 6:18, Paul admonished us to pray "always with all prayer and supplication in the Spirit." Then in 1 Corinthians 14:2, he said, "He who speaks in a tongue does not speak to men but to God, for no one understands him; however, in the spirit he speaks mysteries." When you pray in tongues, you are praying in the Holy Spirit. The Spirit of God prays through you to God, even though your mind cannot understand it. In this way, you can pray always and continually.

Praying in tongues builds and strengthens your inner man and paves the way for victory over the devil. It enables you to pray the perfect will of God and helps you tear down demonic strongholds. Praying in tongues unleashes God's mighty power on your behalf and on behalf of those for whom you are interceding.

You can never pray in tongues too much. When you feel down and defeated, pray in the Spirit. When you think you can't take another step, pray in the Spirit. When you feel like nothing will ever change, pray in the Spirit. Just keep at it. Pray in the Spirit, pray in the Spirit, pray in the Spirit—over and over, over and over. Let the Holy Spirit pray through you, and all of a sudden, you will, as some groups say, "pray through."

What does that mean? It means that as you pray, the Spirit of God wars through you until there is a penetration in the heavenlies. That is your moment of breakthrough, the Holy Ghost moment of victory. You may not see an immediate change in the situation, but you have achieved the spiritual victory which will lead to the actual manifestation. This type of breakthrough often results from praying in tongues.

Binding and Loosing

Praying in the Spirit is one weapon of warfare at your disposal, and binding and loosing is another. You may not be familiar with that term, *binding and loosing,* but it is a very clear principle in Scripture. For example, in Acts 13:9, Paul came against the sorcerer Elymas, who was trying to keep the proconsul from hearing the Gospel. Paul used his authority in Christ to bind the demon power at work. Look at what he said: "O full of all deceit and all fraud, you son of the devil, you enemy of all righteousness, will you not cease perverting the straight ways of the Lord? And now, indeed, the hand of the Lord is upon you, and you shall be blind, not seeing the sun for a time" (vv. 10–11). In this passage, Paul first took authority over (bound) the spirit at work and then pronounced blindness upon the sorcerer (loosed). That's how great his power was.

Jesus Himself spoke on binding and loosing. He said, "How can one enter a strong man's house and plunder his goods, unless he first binds the strong man?" (Matt. 12:29). The devil is the strong man, and until you bind him, you cannot plunder him. You cannot take back what he has stolen until you bind him in Jesus' name. That is a very important tool in spiritual warfare.

Jesus spoke more about our authority to bind and loose in Matthew 16:18–19. After declaring that hell itself could not prevail against His church, Jesus said, "I will give you the keys of the kingdom of heaven, and whatever you bind on earth will be bound in heaven, and whatever you loose on earth will be loosed in heaven" (v. 19).

Jesus said He would give us the keys to the kingdom. A key is a very small thing, but it gives access to something much bigger. When you insert a key into a door, you gain access to an entire house. When you insert a key into the ignition of a car, you activate an engine and can move a vehicle. The key gives you access and is a tool to something much bigger.

The key to the kingdom of God is faith, and faith unlocks the door to spiritual riches and power. In Matthew 17:14–21, Jesus' disciples had been unable to cast a demon out of a boy. When they asked the Lord why they had failed in this, He answered, "Because of your unbelief; for assuredly, I say to you, if you have faith as a mustard seed, you will say to this mountain, 'Move from here to there,' and it will move; and nothing will be impossible for you" (v. 20). Faith is the key that binds the devil and the key to binding the strong man over nations, cities, and individuals.

In verse 21, Jesus added, "However, this kind does not go out except by prayer and fasting." In other words, the loosing ability is found in prayer and fasting. Daniel, for example, through prayer and fasting loosed the archangels Gabriel and Michael to fight on his behalf. Until their power was loosed, Daniel could not achieve victory.

Faith binds, and prayer and fasting looses. They work together as the two keys of the kingdom. Prayer and fasting without faith is fruitless, because faith alone binds, but prayer and fasting looses the power of God and His authority into the situation. When you've got both components working together, you'll find victory against any demon power.

God's greatest desire is to use you as a liberator of the masses. He's given you assurance of your power and ability in Him. He's asking you to open the eyes of the blind, to set at liberty the captives, to proclaim the Year of Jubilee. And He's given you the tools to do it.

God's word to you is clear. Listen to His impassioned plea in Isaiah 43:5–6:

"Fear not, for I am with you;
I will bring your descendants from the east,
And gather you from the west;
I will say to the north, 'Give them up!'
And to the south, 'Do not keep them back!'
Bring My sons from afar,
And My daughters from the ends of the earth."

God is looking for liberators who will command the four corners of the earth, "Give up the souls of men! Give up my brother, son, daughter, wife! Give up my neighbors, coworkers, and friends! Give up, for the Word of God and the blood of the Lamb have set them free." That is the heart of a liberator, and that is the force that prevails against every demon from hell. That is your calling, and that is your destiny.

Until the day that God calls you from this fallen world, you will be engaged in a fierce war with the devil and his demons. They want nothing more than to steal your worship of God and to divert your attention to them and their evil deeds. They will stop at nothing to chip away at the fabric of your spiritual life, and their ultimate goal is to take you to hell with them when you die.

But you are not left to fend for yourself. God keeps you covered as you worship and submit your life to Him. He spreads His garment over you and protects you as you walk in accordance with His principles of divine order. He charges into battle with you as you surge forward with the blood of Jesus, His lovely name, and the Word of God as your banners.

He emboldens you to fight with every fiber of your being as you wage war for your family, finances, and every area of life. He empowers you to violently assail the kingdom of darkness and step confidently into your calling as a liberator. He's ever watching, ever guarding, ever protecting, as He teaches your hands to war.

CPSIA information can be obtained
at www.ICGtesting.com
Printed in the USA
FFOW02n2331070418
46161529-47370FF